PRAISE FOR
FLOURISH BECAUSE

"This book is an inspiration to THRIVING and Surviving through the hard things that life throws at us, some of our own making, some that come from what seem totally out of the blue. Whatever the case, what we do with our challenges truly defines our character and determines our future. A well worthwhile read that I can personally recommend, having seen a lot of it in Kay's personal life experience."

—DONALD CROSBIE, CEO, CFO, Church Pastor/
Minister, Counsellor, Mentor, Life Coach,
World traveler to over 80 countries, Dallas, Texas

"Many times we are not aware of the tragic situations people experience, especially if by all appearances everything seems great: great parents, nice house in the suburbs, golf outings and dinner at the club. This is the backdrop of Kay Whitaker's book, *Flourish Because*. I could pick several adjectives to de scribe my feelings after reading her autobiography. The first that come to mind are intriguing, sad, but also inspiration-al. I'm sure others will have similar feelings with the most prominent being her courage in sharing her story."

—DAN ADAMS, Accredited writer for the documentary
film "Duality – A Graffiti" https://dualityfilm.com/
https://www.imdb.com/title/tt17490336/

"Kay Whitaker is an example of perseverance and strength. I encouraged Kay many years ago to write her story and put it on paper. She did, and we are all blessed and strengthened by her testimony of God's love and mercy."

—GARY CRAWFORD, Retired Funeral Director and Funeral Homeowner, Our Crawford Family of Funeral service for 109 years, Ft. Worth, Texas

Oprah needs to read this book!

"I loved everything about *Flourish Because!* From the trials and tribulations of marriages, raising children, the death of a child, the humorous stories, and how God's love was unwavering in every aspect of Kay's life. Read and enjoy this beautiful, heartwarming book."

—ROSIE KARTALIS, 5.0 out of 5 stars
Top Reader Review from the United States, Amazon.com

Must-read inspirational life story

"We have all had times in our lives when we feel we are up against insurmountable odds. How we respond to those circumstances determines our future. Time and time again Kay was faced with situations where you can make a choice. She always chose to move forward and she was able to do this because of her unwavering faith that Jesus is always there for us. I have known Kay for a long time and thought I knew her well, but this deeply personal story opened my eyes to what a person can overcome in life. It's an inspirational read that everyone can relate too."

—SHARON HORTON, 5.0 out of 5 stars
Top Reader Review from the United States, Amazon.com

Beautiful story of love, life, and redemption
"It lets you know that God wants to write a beautiful story for everyone. Kay lets you know that you can be comforted with the comfort God gave her thru some of her most painful trials...God is faithful!"
—SHARLOTTE CRAWFORD, 5.0 out of 5 stars
Top Reader Review from the United States, Amazon.com

Critical
"Highly recommend this book for young woman. After reading, I've found myself with a brighter perspective."
—MARCELLA HALLMAN, 5.0 out of 5 stars
Top Reader Review from the United States, Amazon.com

Good read!
"I thought I wouldn't gain anything out of this, but it turns out the author and I had a lot in common, and I finished this book feeling encouraged and inspired."
—JACKIE SEPULVEDA, 5.0 out of 5 stars
Top Reader Review from the United States, Amazon.com

Captivating
"Absolutely captivating! Her memoir will help many others and uplift those who need it."
—DIABLO LEYVA, 5.0 out of 5 stars
Top Reader Review from the United States, Amazon.com

Flourishing Because!
"Awesome moving book. A story of life's struggles, all a part of Kay's journey. All used by God. Only God can FLOURISH us on our journey! Very real story and moving and uplifting!"
—SANDY SHERMAN, 5.0 out of 5 Stars;
Top reader review, Amazon.com

A memoir that offers hope and encouragement to fellow women who have faced heartbreaking trials
"I bought and sent a copy to a friend I knew would appreciate the promise of healing and flourishing despite her trials. Well written and full of hope."
—NCE, 5.0 out of 5 Stars; Top reader review, Amazon.com

"Kay's story is truly one of brokenness, sadness, deliverance, and redemption. Through the valley of the shadow of death she has traveled, shaken but not undone, overwhelmed but not cast down. As we've sat with her in the depths of despair over the loss of a child God has shown His faithfulness to her and she stands flourishing today because of a faithful creator who promised to never leave or forsake her. Join her in her journey of unthinkable heartbreak and Joy because Jesus lives."
—ED AND SUSAN JARRETT, Dallas Homebuilder,
TCU supporter and friend, Dallas, Texas

"I have seen the power of God work in and through the life of Kay Whitaker Nelson. She was maid of honor in my wedding on May 30, 1973, and instrumental in leading my late wife of forty-four years, Janice, who was Kay's best friend and college roommate, to the Lord in the fall of 1972. We saw the sovereign hand of God upon her, as she journeyed through life's ups and downs. Kay's life is a story that needed to be told. It will bring hope to anyone who reads it. Janice and I lived this book with Kay and played a part in seeing her fall back into the loving arms of our Savior. This is a book about real life, written by a woman after God's own heart. You will be blessed!"

—JOSH HUFFMAN, Senior National Sales Director, PRIMERICA, Dallas, Texas

"*Flourish Because* is one of the most inspiring, captivating and encouraging books I have ever read. Kay's faith in God shines through the entire book. She lays it all out, the good and the bad. She flourished and overcame many of life's challenges, due to her unwavering faith in God. She honestly shares how Jesus is always there for us, even in the darkest moments. Readers will finish *Flourish Because* feeling encouraged and inspired. She helps us to realize that life is only a step in our journey. I have sent numerous copies to friends who needed uplifting and encouraging. It is wonderfully written, and is a must read for everyone."

—CINDY DEAN, Rancher, and Retired Teacher, Henrietta, Texas

Flourish Because

A Memoir
KAY WHITAKER

Carpenter's Son Publishing

Flourish Because
©2023 Kay Whitaker

Published by Carpenter's Son Publishing, Franklin, Tennessee

Scripture quotations marked (NASB) are taken from the New American Standard Bible®, Copyright © 1960, 1962, 1963, 1968, 1971, 1972, 1973, 1975, 1977, 1995 by The Lockman Foundation
Used by permission. (www.Lockman.org)

Interior Design by Suzanne Lawing

Editing by Ann Tatlock

Printed in the United States of America

978-1-956370-01-0

DEDICATION

In dedicating this memoir, my thoughts linger on the people who shared my life's journey - those who not only endured but flourished amidst its trials and triumphs. I think, most of all, of my children: Christy, Lisa, Johnny, and James.

Christy, Lisa, and Johnny, who continue to walk this earthly realm, have witnessed firsthand the strength and resilience of the human spirit. They have learned from our shared experience that a woman can - and should - resist degrading treatment, that life's status quo can always be challenged. Change, they've realized, can be the salve for life's deepest wounds. I stand in awe of their resilience and their adaptability to the vicissitudes of life, their metamorphosis into emotionally available, forgiving, and responsible adults.

Sadly, James is no longer with us on this mortal plane, yet I find solace in the belief that he's been given a second chance, in a place where the odds are forever in his favor.

There's a profound sense of gratitude that fills me as I observe my children and their journeys. Their narratives are woven with resilience and transformation - tales I hope they will one day share with the world. I bask in the comfort of their successes, in the magnificence of the adults they've become, and in the precious grandchildren they've blessed me with.

Our lives have been marked by unexpected twists, turns, tears, and a fair share of chaos. But through it all, we've learned to navigate the complexities of this journey we call 'life.' We've embraced a mantra, "If you're not FUN, don't come!" and with the grace of God, we've learned to thrive amidst uncertainty.

So here's to flourishing, to growing, to navigating life's labyrinth with grace and courage, to remembering that He is the Way, the Truth, and the Life. This is our story, and I invite you to join us on this journey.

— KAY WHITAKER

FLOURISH IS DEFINED AS:

To grow luxuriantly: THRIVE
To achieve success: PROSPER
To be in a state of activity or production
To reach a height of development or influence
To wield with dramatic gestures
A period of thriving

Contents

PREFACE

On August 1, 2020, ML and I were getting ready to drive to Fort Worth to meet our gun guru, Gary, at the Gun Show at Sid Richardson Exhibition Hall. I had gotten my License to Carry about six months earlier and had been practicing shooting at Eagle Gun Range. I finally decided what gun I liked the best. I was determined to get myself a gun and know how to use it while Donald Trump was still President, because I had no idea what the future held with the opposition party possibly taking our 2nd Amendment rights away from us if they came into office in 2020. In the meantime, the rest of America had the same idea with guns and ammunition in short supply. We met Gary at the entrance, and this guy is somebody everyone needs to meet. He is funny, arrogant in a great way, loves Jesus and has a great relationship with Him. Plus Gary's heart is gigantic! I knew Gary superficially in the old college days at Texas Christian University because he dated my sweet roommate, Kay Crim, from Henderson, Texas. ML got to know and develop a relationship with him after ML and I got married. We would hang out with him and his wife, Sharlotte, at the TCU games tailgating with my college buddies, Janice and Josh. It was through my roommate and best friend Janice and her husband, Josh, that ML and Gary became good friends. At the gun show, we were strolling the aisles and I was getting a little impatient, because I was on a mission and knew what gun I wanted, but these guys kept stopping at the knife displays and a lot of other peripheral displays. I was thinking, "Why are you stopping here?" Finally I told the guys that I was marching forward to find my gun. I eventually came to the last row and saw my gun at a retailer's display. I told the guy to save it for me. It was a Glock 40 and the color was pink. I was thrilled! I ran back to find Gary and ML and told them I found my gun but wanted them to check it out. They followed me to the booth. When Gary saw my choice he said, "Of course a PINK GLOCK! Totally you, KK!" I bought ammo and my new gun that day and was feeling good! After the gun show the three of us went to Angelo's in Fort Worth to eat barbecue. Whenever I've been around Gary the conversation is usually pretty silly and funny, but this day it turned to some serious stuff. We started to talk about our mutual friend, who was my best friend from TCU, Janice. Gary had been a funeral director in Henderson, Texas. When Janice was killed in a very serious car accident on November 14, 2016, the family called Gary in to see if she was in any condition for a viewing. After seeing Janice's charred and mutilated body, he definitely vetoed the idea. So our conversation at the BBQ place was getting serious. Gary looked at me and said, "Kay, I don't know if ML has told you, but he has shared a lot of your life stories with me, and this morning before I came here to meet you and ML I was having my quiet time with the Lord. The Lord told me that when I was with you today I needed to share with you that He wants you to write about all your life experiences, like in a book!" I was bowled over. In all the times I have been around Gary, there never was a serious conversation between the two of us ... now this! I looked at Gary and started crying. He was asking me, "Why are you crying?" I responded, "I have had many people tell me the same thing." Gary asked, "Then why haven't you done it?" That was like asking me why have I been disobeying the Lord for all this time! I told him, "I just thought it was something I didn't want to start because a lot of it I have forgotten and some I didn't want to dig up again. Plus, there is a lot that is just too painful to put on paper." He nodded. Then he started to basically walk me through it. He said, "KK, just start writing, the Lord will guide you through it all. Don't worry about what you're doing, just trust the process. He knows what He wants you to share." So I told Gary, "I'm on it!" I was so encouraged with his positivity and God-led enthusiasm that I could not resist. I guess this is what I needed to kick the can on down the road. So here we are. Since I started writing this, there have been periods where I can't stop writing and then dry periods where I don't want to even think about it. There has always been a pad of paper and pen next to my bed, in Plano and at White Bluff, and there have been many nights when I would wake up and write stories as they came to me.

Thank you, Gary, for your courage and your sensitivity to God's Spirit to get me moving and obeying. It has meant the world to me that you cared this much. It has been a true labor of love and just plain old hard work getting all this into words, much less a book. My prayer and hope is that others out there will see that a life that is open to change can be changed, as I feel that my life has been. I'm so grateful that in my later years I see that God is restoring to me the years the locust took. Sometimes that locust was me and my lousy choices. God's grace is over it all!

Getting older is a really cathartic experience because things in your past life you have chosen to shut out will start to resurface if you let them. If you feel loved and accepted by your Maker, He will give you the courage to go forward and live in freedom and lack of fear. He is the One who gives you the courage to go forward and live in freedom and lack of fear. There is no moving forward in life unless you love yourself. I always did love myself because I had parents and family who were full of love for each other. As I grew, I knew that God the Father, Jesus, His Son and Holy Spirit loved me and accepted me into Their circle. Despite all the "mess-ups" and failures in life I could keep moving forward and not "get stuck" in my messes. I knew I could always find love again.

Every being in the womb is created for love and created by Love, God. In a perfect world, a baby is born, adored and loved and as he or she grows they carry this love to the ones in their lives. This is why love is very important in any person's life. Love creates life in a person, so when life eventually tears one down we can reach deep inside for that life of love we have and keep moving forward.

CHAPTER 1

AWAKENING

... He has said, I will never leave you nor forsake you.

HEBREWS 13:5

The Lord is near to the brokenhearted
and saves those who are crushed in spirit.

PSALM 34:18

The day was May 5, 2010. A beautiful Texas spring day. I was doing what I really love to do, and that is playing golf. I was at Brookhaven Country Club playing in a tournament. I was on hole 11 on the Champs course. I usually don't have my cellphone with me at a tournament but this time I did.

My phone rang and it was my son-in-law, Greg. He asked, "Where are you?" He sounded desperate. I replied, "Playing golf, what's up?" "It's James," he said, "He's in real trouble now and you need to get here as soon as you can." "Where are you and what's going on?" I replied. "I'm here in Fort Worth and James is walking naked on top of a billboard here on 7th

Street. Call Pops and y'all drive over here together. I'll call you back and tell you where to meet the police and they will come and pick you up and bring you to the command unit where we are."

We arrived at the designated place and got into the police car. As we drove to the station, the police officer asked me if I wanted to see James and I said, "No, no, no! Just get us to the command station where my other kids are." When we arrived I ran to the station and didn't dare look up, I was afraid that I would see him on the billboard. There were police cars, reporters, TV cameras and lots of people taking pictures with their cellphones. My adrenaline was flowing rapidly and my heart was racing. As I got into the dimly lit station I saw Lisa, Greg, Johnny and Katie sitting around crying and hugging each other. We all embraced and cried together.

There was a TV in the station with the news story about James on it. I just couldn't watch. I asked Greg what had happened. He said he had talked to Tanson and Kolby, James' best friends and roommates. They told him that James had been struggling with alcohol use from working at a piano bar downtown. Customers buying him shots when he was playing piano, etc. So he quit and he said that really made his boss mad. James grabbed a knife out of the kitchen in their apartment and said, "I am sick of everything and we need to get out of here because they are coming to get us. Tommy is going to kill us!" After an hour of them trying to get him to put the knife down, Tanson tackled James, and Kolby grabbed the knife and got all the knives out of the kitchen. As Tanson was holding James, he kept asking Tanson to kiss him. Tanson kissed James on the lips and James just started crying. At this point, Kolby called Greg, James' brother-in-law. James was settling down, so Tanson let him go. As soon as he did James ran and grabbed a pen and put it to his throat. James ran onto their second-story balcony and jumped over it and started running toward 7th Street. As he was running, they watched and saw that he was shedding his clothes, and then they saw him grab the ladder on the side of the big billboard across the street. As James was climbing it, Tanson called the police.

By the time ML and I got there, James had been on the billboard for three hours. They told me that he was just pacing back and forth on the very top of the 60-foot billboard. I never would look, but ML would watch him, and later he told me that James was fearless. Walking, jumping up and down, looking like a monkey in the trees. I was so afraid he would slip and fall, there was no way I could look. There was a female officer with him and communicating with him to try and coax him down. She asked him about his family and he told her we were all dead. The police kept trying to coax him down but nothing was working. I gathered the kids together and told them we had to pray for the Lord to intervene and get James down off the billboard. So we huddled and prayed, each one of us. "Lord, keep James safe and cause him to come down from this billboard. Let your angels fall all around him and lift him up! In Jesus' powerful name it is done!" It was still a very sunny day and by then he had been up there for four and a half hours. The temperature was in the mid-70s with no breeze. About 30 minutes after praying, we were watching the TV and the weather guy came on to announce that a rainstorm was moving into the Metroplex, followed by a cold front. We all looked at each other and were thinking, "Is this the answer to our prayers?" Sure enough, within 40 minutes the clouds started rolling in and the wind started blowing. In Texas there is a saying: "Just wait around five minutes and the weather will change!" The temp dropped some and the rain started. James, I was told, was curled up sitting on the billboard once the rain started. As it was raining the temperature quickly dropped into the 60s, with the wind increasing. The police could tell James was getting really cold. The policewoman who had been talking to James told him to come down. "It's too cold up there and I have a blanket here for you." That is all it took. Just some help from Almighty God to get James to come down. They say that James shinnied down that pole like a monkey. They placed the blanket around him and put him in the back of the police car.

The police came into the station to announce to us that James was safely down and in the police car and asked us if we would like to see him before they took him to the hospital.

We were crying, hugging, praising and thanking God for answering our prayers. Once again James is rescued. We all said, "Yes, we want to see him!"

Literally, all we got to do was wave to him in the back of the police car as they slowly drove by. He turned his head and raised his arms to wave. We all waved back through our tears. As he looked back, I saw the strangest thing. James' neck, as he craned to look back at us, looked twice as long as normal and his eyes looked deranged and demonic. It was so scary to me. I will never forget the look. As he drove off, the policewoman looked at us and said, "Well, thank God that is over and he is okay."

I thought to myself, "Oh no, this is not over, it is just the beginning!"

At that moment, the future was a big blank slate.

CHAPTER 2

THE BEGINNING

... there is but one God, the Father, from whom are all things, and we exist for Him; and one Lord, Jesus Christ, by whom are all things and we exist through Him.

1 CORINTHIANS 8:6

I was raised with very supportive and kind parents. From my early childhood, I knew that God was very important.

Mom shares with me that when I was around four years of age, at bedtime I would look up at her and say, "Mom, God is very important." This was before my mom had even accepted the Lord. But in my spirit was the recognition of His Spirit. The wonderful love and acceptance of kind parents really helps to keep a child's heart tender so the Spirit can be accepted. How little I knew how much this mighty God would influence my life and the responses I would have to what life brought my way. This book is His story for me and I want to share this with all His children to demonstrate that no matter what happens to you during your time here on this earth you will find that He is always there for you despite your good and/or bad choices.

Let's start at the beginning.

I was the first born in 1952 to a sweet small-town couple, only 19 years old, who had been "childhood sweethearts" since eighth grade in Throckmorton, Texas. After graduating from high school they ended up marrying one year later when they were 19 years old. Dad was a geology major and a freshman quarterback at TCU in Fort Worth in 1950 on an athletic scholarship. I was born on February 12, 1952 in Fort Worth to these two youngsters. We lived on Waits Street in Fort Worth, and Dad ended up getting his master's degree in geology. Mom told me that when I was born she considered me her "Baby" as in a baby doll. She was so excited to have a baby girl. As I got older, Mom told me that she loved having a baby and to this day my mom is crazy about infants, especially her great-grandbabies. A couple of years later my brother, Russell, was born.

The oil business led my dad from Fort Worth to the oil patch in Midland as a newly hired Texaco geologist. This was a great time for my dad because it was a huge period of exploration for a geologist. He was gone a lot on well sites to keep analyzing the week's seismic readings. He was missed, especially by my mom, who had two wild toddlers at home all by herself. Many times she did get relief when Dad's mom and dad came from Throckmorton to help her out. They were my Grandma and Granddad Whitaker, whom I was crazy about. All I really remember from Midland were the tarantulas and the mimosa switches my mom and dad used to switch us with to keep us out of the street. And there were a couple of tornadoes I remember seeing through our big plateglass windows. Dad would point out the tornadoes in the distance, but thank God they never touched our home. We moved a lot because my dad was a geologist. Dad followed where the oil patch led us. After Midland we moved to Amarillo, Texas. I started first grade and completed second grade at Wolflin Elementary School. My dad started a new job with an oil company out of Denver, Colorado. Hamilton Brothers became my dad's next employer and it was the best career decision he ever made. It was in Amarillo that my little sister Cheryl was born in 1959. We had a cute bungalow house on Ong Street very near my school. I walked to and from school every day. Life was so carefree and happy. I had made a lot of new friends between church and school.

After a little more than two years, Dad's new company wanted him to move to Calgary, Alberta, Canada. Away we went, with the Mayflower moving van going on ahead of us and filling up our station wagon for the long haul to Calgary. Dad decided to make it a long vacation, so we drove north and saw all the sights between Amarillo, Texas and Calgary, Canada. In the next two weeks we saw Colorado, Wyoming and Montana. We saw the Rockies, the Grand Tetons, lots of buffalo and bears. I can't imagine how many times we asked our parents, "Are we there yet?" In those days we didn't have seat belts, so we were rolling around and fighting all over the back seat. I don't know how they did it, but we eventually got to Calgary and settled into the first of three homes we would have in Calgary for our 18 months or so there. The first home we moved into was a big Victorian two-story that my parents rented from another man who knew Dad through the oil business. We all loved it because it was very big and located in an old neighborhood near downtown with lots of yard and big trees to play in. Since we were new to the area, my mom was grateful that the owners of the house left her lots of local information so she wouldn't be so lost in this "foreign country!" My brother and I were around eight and six. We got to Calgary in June and Russell and I were outside from morning to dusk, which happened about 11 PM! We had lots of fun adventures riding bikes and seeing all the birds in the yard. We moved in around the time of nesting and lots of baby birds were being born. Russell and I made it our job to take care of all the baby birds that had fallen out of their nests.

Much to my mom's chagrin, Russell and I would rescue many of these nestlings we found on the ground. I do remember the birds and taking care of them. However, Mom remembers some pretty funny stories about things we did to keep them alive. One night she came in to kiss me goodnight and I was already asleep. After she kissed me, she noticed a cord coming out from under the closet door. When she opened it she saw that we had put a nest with a couple of nestlings in the closet with a heating pad on, keeping them nice and toasty. That came to a screeching halt the next morning. There was also the time when we were going to go to the picture show and see the new Walt Disney movie, *Snow White*. I asked my mom if I could take some baby birds with me to the show. Of course, the answer was no. But in the theater, Mom heard this subdued tweeting close by. She looked around, suspecting me. Mom had me hand her my little purse and, sure enough, there were the two little nestlings chirping inside. She says that she could not help but smile!

We had lots of adventures in the wild Rockies. We would take weekend trips to Banff and visit the Indian reservations. There were real Indians in teepees and campfires in their campsite. The men and women wore authentic Indian apparel. It was so cool. I can especially remember an area called Lake Louise. I truly remember the beauty of my Father's world in Canada.

When we first moved to Calgary, it was then and there, in a small Southern Baptist church, that I asked Jesus to come into my heart. I cried and cried when I realized He would make me "white as snow." When I would close my eyes at night as a child, I would see all this ugly black stuff and I would always pray for the Lord to make me white and soft. This is what He did to my heart when I said yes to Him. I also loved reading the Bible. I was fortunate enough to always have sweet, loving Sunday school teachers. Speaking of teachers, as a little girl from Texas I had some really sweet old ladies as my first and second grade teachers in Amarillo. When we moved to Calgary, that all changed. I was in an elementary school in Calgary and my third grade teacher's name was Mrs. Noble and boy, was she grim. I can remember how strict she was on keeping all her rules. I can't tell you how many times I ended up in isolation in the coat room for talking too much. I still don't get that because I didn't really know anyone. But the biggie with Mrs. Noble was her "eraser rule." At the beginning of each month, she would give each of us 20 kids a small square of an eraser. I'll bet it was only a half-inch on all surfaces. I really didn't get it. Was this her rule so we would not make so many mistakes or what? I can't tell you how many times I had to tell Mrs. Noble that I ran out of my eraser or

I got so scared of her that I actually *didn't* tell her. I would just draw a line through my mistake and correct it. Once she realized my infraction, it was off to the coat room for me ... again. I didn't look forward to going to that school every day. After this school we moved out west of Calgary on the road to Banff. We had a great house in the country with big picture windows and views of the Canadian Rockies. I was so glad to try a new school. This was a country school with four school rooms and three grades in each classroom ... kind of like the old proverbial "one-room schoolhouse." The students were mostly children of ranchers and farmers in the area. I was in the fourth grade at this school. So I was in the classroom with fourth- to sixth-graders. Russell was in the first through third grade classroom. There was one bus that would pick all of us up and take us to the school. My teacher was so nice. She had to teach three grade levels. Looking back, it had the feel of a large family homeschool experience. The older students would help the younger ones. I can remember walking to the bus stop from our house. The walk was about a hundred yards. In the warmer days it was so fun. In the cold Canadian winter it was tortuous. I can remember a photo Dad took of me and Russell walking to the bus with all our layers and our Eskimo Hudson Bay parkas on. As we walked, the wind was so strong that in the pictures our bodies are actually leaning due to the gusts of wind. Kind of a nice different schooling experience in the Calgary countryside. We also had some wonderful experiences in the summer living in the country. We would watch out the big picture windows in the back of the house and see these big guinea pig-looking animals running around all over and then scurrying down their holes in the ground for refuge. Russell and I had the great idea of catching these guys, just for the sake of catching them. We got a couple of Mom's rectangular plastic basins, some string, sturdy sticks and lots of popcorn. We would tilt the basins up with the sticks and put popcorn on the ground leading from their holes to the pile of popcorn inside the basin. On the stick we tied pieces of the twine. We would hide behind the bushes with the string in our hands and wait. I can remember how exhilarating the wait was for us. Inevitably, a "prairie dog" would come along. We eventually found out these weren't guinea pigs. BAM! We would pull the string and down the basin would come and trap the prairie dog. We would laugh and get so excited. The prairie dog would rattle around inside the basin and we would sit on the top of the basin to keep it from getting out. Eventually we would lift one end of the basin off and it would scurry to his refuge hole.

In the early 1960s, a family from Texas was an oddity to the Canadians. I can remember two events that kind of showed how different our culture and language were. The first is when I was at a friend's birthday party and they wanted us to sit on the "Chesterfield." I said, "No thanks," because I thought a Chesterfield was an American cigarette. But when I heard that a Chesterfield was a sofa, I confessed I misunderstood. Another instance was at a party they asked who wanted "jam" with their cake and I responded, "No thanks." All I could think was my Grandma's plum jam. Then I found out that the jam was really Jell-O. There were many episodes of teasing us about our accent and word choices compared to the Canadians. I actually found it fun because, mainly, we were just so proud to be from Texas. It was time to move on to new friends and new places.

Because we did move so much while I was growing up, I learned to adapt and make lots of new friends wherever we went. I never remember feeling bad or left out when I would be in a new school and be the "new kid." It was like an adventure to see what new friends I would make. Being outgoing and friendly helped me out a lot also.

When we left Calgary, this Texas girl was so excited to come back to America.

CHAPTER 3

KEEP MOVING.
WHERE NOW?

Be anxious for nothing, but in everything with prayer and
supplication with thanksgiving let your requests be made
known to God. And the peace of God, which passes all com-
prehension, shall guard your hearts and minds in Christ Jesus.

PHILIPPIANS 4:6-7

On our next move, we didn't end up back in Texas after all, but
instead Mississippi. We moved to Jackson where I would be
in the second semester of fourth grade. Jackson has a special
place in my heart. Even to this day whenever I have a good
dream, the setting is usually somewhere in Jackson. We lived
in Jackson from my fourth grade to the summer of eighth
grade. My social life was wonderful with great friends, schools
and a great church. We were there during some of America's
darkest moments. I was in sixth grade when Kennedy was
assassinated and we saw the civil rights movement start in
Mississippi. But in my sixth grade brain, to me life was good

because we got to live there longer than anywhere else we had ever lived.

The one event that did cast a dark cloud over my joyful days in Jackson was the day my little sister, Cheryl, went missing. It was a beautiful September Sunday morning in 1963. We had just moved into a development in Jackson to a new home. This particular regular Sunday morning started as usual. We all rose at seven in the morning and were getting ready for church. We noticed that Cheryl, who was four at the time, was nowhere around and her bed was empty. We also noticed that our dogs were missing. So we slowly began to panic. This is every parent's nightmare and it was happening to my parents, my brother and myself. We started looking all over the neighborhood and calling out her name. Since it was a new development, there were only two other houses on our street. Lots of wooded areas all around us. Across the street we had the Primos family compound and up the street we had the Apostle family lots. After a couple of hours with no hints of Cheryl, my dad called the police. They asked a lot of questions and got some of her clothes so the bloodhounds would have a scent. They also called in trustees from the state prison to search all the wooded property. Right behind our lot was a large pond, which they dragged looking for her body. This was getting really scary and serious. As you can guess, there was a lot of drama at home with a lot of tears and fear. There were helicopters, airplanes and horseback officers looking for her. The Jackson Police, Hinds County Sheriff's office and the National Guard were participating. It seemed to me that the whole city, county and state were involved in looking for Cheryl. I called on my church friends to pray for us and for us to find Cheryl alive and well. Our church, Broadmoor Baptist, was all over our prayer requests and what was happening. Our pastor came over along with a lot of other people. The phone was ringing off the wall. The local TV channels were covering it, so friends were finding out about this and wanted us to know they were praying. All we could do as a family was just stay close to each other in the house while the police kept us posted on what was going on. I can remember going to my bedroom to be alone and looking out my front window and seeing all the prison trustees in their white jumpsuits combing all the wooded areas looking for her. After all this happened, the Cuban Missile Crisis occurred and there was such a fear of the Russians invading. I would have nightmares of the Russians coming up through the wooded areas to our house just like I was seeing these trustees coming up the hill to our home.

Cheryl had been missing for almost eight hours when the police got a call from a man who said he had her at his home and she was fine. It turns out that Cheryl, being the dog lover that she is, woke up before all of us and followed our dog, Rebel, and Rinty, our neighbors' dog, into the woods, and she just kept following them until she couldn't walk anymore because of all the stickers. She ended up in a wooded area near my junior high school. To get to where she ended up, she had to walk under a freeway about three miles from our home. The man who found her was out in the woods with his son looking for insects for a science project and they saw her asleep sitting up against the tree with the dogs' heads on her lap asleep as well. He asked her what she was thinking when she couldn't get back home and she said, "I just wished I was

Peter Pan so I could fly home!" He took her to his home, fed her and called the police. In the meantime, the Governor of Mississippi and the Mayor of Jackson were now at our home waiting for the homecoming. There were about a hundred people in our yard when she came home. When she got back to our house, in the arms of my crying dad, we covered her with kisses and hugs and gave thanks to our heavenly Father who had been watching over her.

If this had happened in 2020, it would probably not have turned out so well. To this day, I still love Jackson because the people there were so kind and I have never felt a community spirit anywhere else I have lived like I felt there.

After the trauma of Cheryl being lost, life returned to normal. Mom and Dad went back to their plane trips. They flew to Mazatlán, Mexico. My dad loved this vacation spot. Whenever they would go, they would get Lucille, our maid, to come stay and babysit us. This was a total joke. I was in the seventh grade at this time and totally had learned how to drive from my grandma. So of course when Lucille was taking her daily naps on my dad's recliner, my girlfriends and I were driving all over Jackson, Mississippi in my mom's baby blue Buick LeSabre!

During our time in Jackson, Dad still was gone a lot for work. Looking back on my life and its chaos, I truly believe that to have a dad who is home and participates in the activities of a child helps to ground the child. My brother and I were the two who were not around Dad much growing up in our elementary and middle school years. Whereas my sister, who was seven years younger, grew up with Dad around a whole lot more during those years when he did less traveling.

There were some advantages to all of Dad's being gone for work, though. It reaped a lot of financial advantages for all of us later on in life. I was still so fortunate to have parents who were both loving, accepting and fun.

I was loving my junior high years at Chastain Junior High. I loved all my classes and teachers and made great friends. I had never gotten involved in any sport until the tennis coach at Chastain asked me to try out for the tennis team my eighth grade year, and I made it. Back in my day there were very few sports for girls and no sports outside of school for females. So we were pretty much limited. But tennis was a good opportunity for me to compete and learn a new sport. My coach's name was Coach White. He was so encouraging to me as a coach and I truly excelled in tennis. He was a very tough training coach and I really appreciated that because it made me work so hard. I would play tennis for the next 30 years of my life.

About a year later, I was flying high with friends and school and preparing to try out for ninth grade cheerleader. Our family was driving home from church and all three of us kids were sitting in the back seat. I was sitting behind my dad. Dad turned around and looked at Russell and Cheryl and he said, "Who wants to move back to Texas?" I didn't say anything but they yelled, "YEAH!" I couldn't believe this was happening. I still didn't say anything. I kept thinking, "I'm in eighth grade and trying out to be a freshman cheerleader at Murrah High School ... I don't want to move to Texas." When we got home I ran to my room, slammed the door and started crying. Then I got on my bike and rode to my friend Laurie's house to cry some more. I would have driven the Buick LeSabre if my parents hadn't been home!

It happened in July of 1966. We packed up the car and the Mayflower truck showed up. We headed west to Houston. It was a very sad day for me. Mayflower had come and gone once again. When we got to Houston, we had to live in an apartment while our new home was being finished. Looking back at that time, I got a little depressed because there was no one I knew there and I was crushed to have to leave Jackson. So that summer was spent with family and some of my time was in Throckmorton, Texas staying with my grandparents. Thankfully, I had friends there.

CHAPTER 4

HOME AWAY FROM HOME

The Lord's lovingkindnesses indeed never cease, for His compassions never fail. They are new every morning.

LAMENTATIONS 3:22-23

My times in Throckmorton were so wonderful to me because my paternal grandparents always made me feel so special. I would have to say that my grandma, Edna, made a big impression in my life. She was raised near Woodson, Texas in the early 1900s and was her daddy's favorite. She was raised on an old-fashioned farm and everyone was full of old-fashioned sayings about everything in life. She was a little redheaded girl who spent many hours and days picking cotton with her old-fashioned fabric sunbonnet on, and no sunscreen on since it hadn't been invented yet. You can imagine what her skin's future was. She taught me so many great things about taking care of a household and cooking. When my brother and I would go to stay with them during the summer, I would stay out of the hot Texas heat and help Grandma take care of the domestic front. While my brother, much to his chagrin, would follow Granddad out to take care of the cows or whatever was waiting for them out in the burning Texas sun on the "place." Russell would always complain when Granddad would rouse him at five in the morning so they could go to the local cafe for breakfast and "chew the fat" with the cowboys. Russell would complain so much about how tired he was and my granddad's famous retort was, "I can't make you go to bed at night, but in the morning I can sure make you wish you did! Now git up!"

I also remember my first encounter with Texas horny toads was in Throckmorton. On those hot and very dry days as kids, Russell and I and our local friends would catch as many horny toads as we could. We would catch big daddy toads, momma toads and baby toads. We would build little houses out of mud for these reptiles and create fences from rocks so they couldn't get out of their home pens. Lots of fun, and little did I know that the Horned Frogs of TCU were in my future.

Being a fifth-generation Texan, there are a lot of old-timer stories passed down by the older folks. Every year growing up, we always went to Throckmorton for the Whitaker Reunion. Recently I have been really into Ancestry.com like many of my cousins and I am grateful that I have learned so much about my family's five generations of Texas history. At our Whitaker reunions, the patriarchs and matriarchs would tell great stories about the days of the Comanche Indians and our relatives' dealings with them on the Texas plains. We have had these reunions every second Sunday in June since way before I was born. We went almost every year, except our year in Calgary. Our line of Whitakers settled mostly in Throckmorton County starting in the late 1800s. I have a great-grandmother named Sarah Elizabeth Massengill Whitaker. She died in 1964, so I have some very clear memories of her. She was born in 1871 during the Wild West and the Indian days of Texas.

Her life was typical for that time. Her mother died when she was very young and her ranching dad would take her with him on the Chisholm Trail cattle drives where she would cook for the cowboys. It was a rough life full of hard work for a 14-year-old. By the time I met "Ma" she was getting on up there in years and kind of scared me. When I was a little girl of eight, Ma would call me to come closer and sit on her lap. At that point in my young life, I would look up and see Ma's whiskers, her glass eye and the snuff spittle can next to her and would basically run outside. She was quite a character. She had five girls and five boys which she and Pa raised on a farm in Woodson, Texas. She lost one of her girls to burn injuries as a young child. I definitely had some really interesting characters in great aunts, uncles, and a passel of first, second and third cousins. It was and is a great experience. The great thing about being able to touch and be so near your roots is that it gives you a grounding as to who you are, which you have a hard time finding without family ties. I'm just grateful to be a part of such a loving extended and fun family. When I was 13, I learned how to drive a car. My Grandma Whitaker taught me. I would drive her into town to shop. She became totally blind by the time she was 50. She started teaching me to drive because she wanted me to take her to Kirksey's grocery store in Throckmorton. We would go every day and I loved how she trusted me. I would help her get into her seat and off we would go. She taught me how to lead her when we were walking in places she was not familiar with. I did this for her until the day she died. I would follow her around and do what she told me to do when we were at the house. By 10 in the morning all the groceries were bought, laundry done and put away. In fact, I got some training most kids don't get. Since Texas summers are so hot, the ranchers always wore "khakis." These khakis were heavy-duty cotton long sleeve shirts and long pants. I never could figure out how they could wear those in the Texas heat. Back in the day, all the ironing and laundry were done at home. So I learned how to starch the khakis, hang them out to dry, then bring them in and sprinkle them with water and roll them up, and then put them in a plastic zippered bag for a while to soak up the water. Next step was the hardest part. The iron was very hot and if you ironed the khakis the correct way, the steam and the starch made for an excellent ironing project. I was always so proud when my ironing pleased my grandma. I don't know how she could do so much and be so blind, but she did. She was amazing and I was glad that Throckmorton had become our home base. Grandma was from the school of "hard work breeds prosperity." Grandma would have a full breakfast early morning before sunrise for the cowboys, except when they went to the cafe, and then a full multi-course "dinner" at noon with multiple desserts to choose from. Six o'clock suppertime was suppertime with a lighter course of scrambled eggs or leftovers.

My grandma had a degenerative eye disease called retinitis pigmentosa. She was not diagnosed until after marrying my granddad, when she was around 20. When they were first married, Grandma said that if she had to get up in the middle of the night it was always pitch black to her and she would stumble around. One night early in their marriage Granddad asked her, "Edna, what is going on?" She said, "Well, it is night and dark and I can't see anything." Granddad told her that the moonlight was shining into their room, but she said it was still pitch black to her. She said she never remembered seeing anything once the sun went down. He took her to an ophthalmologist in Fort Worth in the 1940s where she was diagnosed. Grandma told me she always feared she would pass this disease on to me, especially after I had to start wearing glasses when I was 10 from nearsightedness. But I have remained free from that. I was always very close to Grandma. She was my best friend as a young girl. My granddad was much more strict with me, but I never had any doubt that he would do anything for me. I think that since my dad was their only child and we were their only grandchildren, they spoiled us a bit. I feel very blessed to have that bond with them.

CHAPTER 5

FUN TIMES AHEAD

The steps of a man are established by the Lord; and He delights in his way. When he falls, he shall not be hurled headlong; because the Lord is the One who holds his hand.

PSALM 37:23-24

Once school started and we were in our new home in Houston in September of 1966, I went to Memorial High School in the Spring Branch area. I was overwhelmed with the crowded school. Being in the ninth grade in a school that had ninth through twelfth grades, we freshmen were the runts. Mom has told me that she was concerned about me during that time we lived in the apartment. She thought that I was getting depressed because I was eating more than usual for me and staying in my room for longer times. But this quickly resolved itself as I started getting social at school. As usual, I met a lot of new friends and started going to slumber parties and having fun again. My freshman year was full of school spirit and lots of crazy fun!

The next year a bunch of us left Memorial to go to the newest high school in the district. Westchester was the new school and we all had a mission. To make it a great school! It was at Westchester that I really became involved. I ended up on the drill team. Our one goal for the next three years was to beat Memorial, our arch rival. We finally did beat them in football our senior year, which was a great year because I got to be a cheerleader during all the wonderful victories that year when we were the underdog! It really created a great bond for a school as big as we were, and our school spirit was out of the park! Another fun time for me during high school was my 16th birthday. It was February 1968. Dad and Mom took me and my boyfriend, Frank, to go eat in downtown Houston at the swanky Petroleum Club. It sat on top of the Republic Bank building. We had a wonderful dinner and they gave me a beautiful new watch for my birthday present. I was so grateful and having a wonderful time. The curtain on the stage opens and out walks Frankie Valli and the Four Seasons! What? This was the surprise of the season! I was ecstatic! How did Dad keep this a secret? They were my favorite band at the time. "Can't Take My Eyes Off You!" We were so close to the guys I could have touched them! So needless to say, after getting the watch I thought the night was over but it lasted hours longer with this wonderful band entertaining us all. I lived this day out forever and here I am sharing it now. Thanks Dad! You really knew how to start a party.

My spiritual life really took off in high school. I was very involved with Young Life and Navigators Bible Study. I grew so much in my faith and loved to share my faith with my classmates. I was a huge history buff and read a lot. During my junior year, my mom got to know one of the history teachers at Westchester, Mrs. Palmer, at a Bible study. They started talking about maybe asking the school if Mrs. Palmer could teach a year class on the Bible for credit. It was a long shot, but it was approved. So in the fall of 1969, Westchester High School had a full history credit in the study of the Bible. I think it only lasted one year, but it was invaluable for all of us who took the class. There were a bunch of us who loved the Lord and studied together.

In the fall of 1969, a group from the Children of God came to my high school campus and talked to us during our lunch break in the courtyard outside. Two of my girlfriends and I were approached by two guys who invited us to come to their camp, which was at Bear Creek Park just west of the school. So after school we headed to the camp in one car. They greeted us and told us we were going to learn so much. As soon as we set foot in the camp, I started getting a creepy feeling because everyone had the real live "hippy" look. Every tent had a campfire and it was a really primitive environment. They took us into a dimly lit tent and we all sat on the ground in a circle. They started sharing their religion and what they believed about life. Then they asked us if we wanted to speak in tongues. We were like "sure." I didn't even know what that meant. They would stand over us and lay hands on our shoulders and chant with strange noises. From then on it felt like they were trying to brainwash us and I was wanting to get out of there. I whispered to my girlfriend, "Let's go!" We told them thank you and got into our car and left. Later on we found out that one of our classmates, whom I didn't know, went out there also. But his ending wasn't so great. He left with them and his mother never saw him again.

They dropped me off at my home and my dad was at the doorway waiting for me ... mad as a hornet! Little did I know that my Young Life Bible study teacher had called my parents to inform them of where we had gone. Dad had been out there looking for us when we were in the tent. He said he knew where I had been and couldn't believe I would be so stupid to go out to someplace with such dangerous people. He was so mad that he actually told me to lean over the bed and he pulled out his belt and he whipped me. I couldn't believe it. I hadn't gotten a "whupping" since I was probably six years old! He was so frightened for my safety. I talked to my other friends who also went and I was the only who got a whupping! Once again the Lord was watching over me and keeping me safe. My years at Westchester were memorable with lifelong relationships.

One particular family vacation comes to mind that happened the summer of my graduation in 1970. My dad loved taking us on vacations to Mazatlán, Mexico, but this year he was taking us all to Puerto Vallarta with a side trip to San Blas, because according to my surfer brother, Russell, they had the best surf and he and his buddy wanted to try it. Dad was okay with that. He told us that we would spend a week in Puerto Vallarta and then rent some cars and head north to San Blas about a three-hour drive from Puerto Vallarta. I took my friend Patti and Russ took his buddy Scott. We flew to Puerto Vallarta and had a fabulous week at this great seaside hotel with amazing food. We were all careful what we ate so as not to catch "Montezuma's Revenge." We had all had it at least once. It was not fun. Time in this wonderful place came to an end and it was time to head north to San Blas, which none of us had heard of except my brother. We rented an open-air Jeep and a sedan. Now mind you, we had luggage for seven people and two large surfboards to load into these two automobiles, plus have a place for us to sit. We looked like the Beverly Hillbillies heading into California with everything piled up and loaded down. There was lots of laughter with this group and teasing. Dad drove the Jeep and Mom drove the sedan behind him. We literally went through jungles with lots of hills and rough terrain. There weren't a lot of gas stations on the way, so lots of potty stops on the side of the road. It took us three hours to get to the village. Before we took this detour to San Blas, my dad had gotten a brochure about a great hotel in San Blas that had pictures of the hotel and the beach. He booked it and as we took off, we thought we would be okay in that hotel and the surf would make Russell happy. As we got closer to San Blas, we were noticing that there was little traffic or commerce … no "turistas." There was a strong feeling of trepidation as we entered the outskirts of the village. There was silence in the car as Patti, my sister, Mom and I were following Dad and slowly driving up this well-worn, winding dirt path. Going to Mexico in the 1960s wasn't as scary as going today. There was not the cartel and crime problems that are so rampant now. There were drug problems throughout Mexico, though, but just not as scary. As we rode in the Jeep, I was quickly reminded of two guys I knew from high school that had gotten so hooked on drugs that they headed to Mexico to keep up their habits and died in Mexico before graduating from high school.

As we were approaching this village, all we saw were the local women cleaning and beating their wet clothes on rocks in this flowing creek running through the area. I was beginning to be afraid and I could tell all of us were. I'm sure my dad was thinking, "Maybe this was not such a good idea." Because I sure was! We finally came to what looked like the village square with a few vendors and goods to sell. In the center at the end of the square was the local Catholic Church. I can only imagine what the locals thought when they saw this entourage of "gringos." We stopped. We all got out. Dad told us to stay in the village and walk around, and maybe do some shopping. There was enough adventure in me and Patti that we wanted to go check out the church. Off we went, and it was so creepy. It had all the traditional Catholic symbols everywhere and candle-lighting was going on by the locals, who were constantly staring at us. I knew enough Spanish to be friendly with small talk. We looked to the center at the front of the church and saw a glass crypt. We walked up to it and looked down to see that there was a real human cadaver that was rotting away. It was covered by the glass and had some brightly colored covering over it. We had no idea who this was and why it was right in the middle of this little cathedral. We were so scared and left quickly to go find Mom and Cheryl, who were shopping at one of the vendors. They both were holding a Coca-Cola. Patti and I ran to get one for ourselves. In the meantime, we just sat and waited for Dad and the boys to return to the square. No one approached us for money or anything. I was surprised because today young children are all over tourists for money in many third-world countries. We certainly knew we were in a third-world village here. Dad and the boys returned and told us they wanted to take us to our hotel on the beach. We were relieved and as we approached we kept waiting to see a building. Dad stopped and said, "See that sign over there?" We saw it and he said that it was a small billboard out front of our supposedly built hotel. All we saw were stilts with nothing on top and swamps everywhere. There was no beach, but Dad said that Russell and Scott had gotten out to surf and couldn't stand it because they got eaten up by mosquitos. At this point, Dad said we have to go back to the village and hopefully get something to eat and a place to stay. After what we had seen in the village, Patti and I just looked at each other and rolled our eyes. Once in the village, Dad found a small cafe. Off we headed to eat. As we were approaching the cafe, we noticed that there was a small moat around it with planks going across to provide a walkway to get into the cafe. As we were looking down at the moat, we saw alligators. Then we saw some of the cooks throwing the trash into the moat and the alligators were all over it. I guess they were the cafe's garbage disposal. This was one of my scariest tourist moments, as we all were feeling the same thing. We all were safely sitting down at the table and the waiter brought us Cokes and white bread. He also brought out some beautiful freshly caught lobsters and tried to ask us if we wanted them to eat. Of course we all said, "Si, Senor!" Dad said this was the best we could eat and try to avoid the "Montezuma's Revenge." I really don't think I have had lobster that tasted better than that freshly caught lobster, and I was so hungry!

We were all shocked at how delicious the lobster was with our white bread and Cokes. Of course there was no ice, but we were grateful that we weren't starving anymore.

After making it back over the alligator moat, we headed to what someone had pointed out to Dad as the hotel. It was now around late afternoon and we all walked into this sultry lobby with a stoned guy sitting in the corner of the small entry sleeping it off. Dad got us two rooms, one for the girls and one for the guys. We unloaded as little of our cargo as possible and headed up the stairs to what we hoped would be a decent night's sleep. As we got up the stairs, we took a left turn and saw that we were on an outside balcony with what looked like an old pool below the balcony. This place was so run down and the pool was just seething with moss and who knows what else. We didn't see anyone else in this place except the stoned guy and the hotel owner. We got to our room doors and of course there were no locks. As we walked in, what we saw was startling. Of course the room was small, but it did have two full-size mattresses sitting on top of rickety springs. In the middle of the room, a light bulb hung from a single wire in the ceiling. Over to the side was a small toilet/shower area. There was a small shower that did have water coming out, but no one was willing to try it out. Who knew what kind of deadly microbes were lurking in that shower. The lighting was crude. As the sun was going down, we tried our light, and it did work for a while. Dad came over and told us that their room was in the same dilapidated and deteriorated condition. He was furious that he had gotten hoodwinked into booking rooms in a hotel that didn't even exist. It was time for us to get some rest, so we settled down in our beds. Patti and

I started singing, "We Are One in the Spirit" and Mom and Cheryl chimed in. I think this gave us a sense of protection because, like I said, there were no locks on any of the doors. I don't know how, but I did fall asleep for a bit, then we woke up hearing Mom in the bathroom with Cheryl, who ended up with … Montezuma's Revenge. She was up and down with diarrhea for most of the night. In the meantime, there came a monsoon rainstorm as we were trying to resume some sleep. The roof on this upstairs room was made of thin metal sheets. The rain started coming into the room, not with a drip here and there but water everywhere. We were totally drenched. Finally the rain let up and you could feel that sunrise was coming. Dad knocked on our door and said, "We are out of here, right now!" So we hurriedly got what little we had in the rooms and loaded up the car, just grateful that we survived this. As we were getting into the car heading down the muddy village dirt road, Mom pointed out to us to listen to the rooster crowing in the background. As Mom says, "This was our vacation from hell!" Thankfully we made it back home okay.

As I entered my senior year, it was time to decide where to go to college. I was dating my high school boyfriend, Frank. He was going to Tulane on a football scholarship and wanted me to follow him, but I just never could see myself in New Orleans. He wasn't happy with that but that was how I felt. In the end, I decided to go to TCU in Fort Worth, where my dad had gone, not too far from Houston and close to my grandparents in Throckmorton. So after four years in Houston, it was time to start over again as a freshman in college. I went through rush and pledged Chi Omega. I also took "pot luck" on my roommate. She was a sweet girl, also named Kay, from

Henderson, Texas. A good friend from high school and my partner from the "Vacation from Hell," Patti, was at TCU with me. We decided not to room together but take "pot luck" and just see who the Lord put us with!

I was still "going with" Frank during that first fall semester. I would fly to New Orleans to see him play football and check out Tulane. He really wanted me to transfer to Sophie Newcomb and be with him. I finally said I would and started the transfer process. My parents were furious and did not want me to do this. I had conflicting feelings about it. I wanted to make them happy and I wanted to make Frank happy too. Over the holidays after first semester, Frank and I broke up because I just didn't think the Lord wanted me to transfer to Sophie Newcomb. I had been accepted to Sophie Newcomb and had unenrolled at TCU, so I was ready to go in January and be with him, but I never had a good feeling about it. Over the Christmas break, I spent so much time with him talking about it and him trying to convince me to go, and the rest of the time I spent with my parents trying to talk me out of going to New Orleans. Ultimately, I decided to go back to TCU. Frank and I broke up. It was a very sad thing because it really felt so final. In the last four years of high school we had lots of breakups and reunions, but this time it felt truly over. I ended up getting back into TCU and was rooming with Kay again and hanging with Patti.

When I came back to TCU for the second semester, I enrolled in Geology 101 and the professor was Dr. Dan Jarvis. I kept thinking that name sounded so familiar, but being a dingy freshman I blew it off. During roll call the professor was calling out peoples' names present or not. After the roll call was over, Dr. Jarvis asked, "Is there anyone whose name I didn't call?" I had been talking and didn't even hear that he had called out my legal name, Marjorie Kay Whitaker. I raised my hand. I said, "Sir, you didn't call my name!" He said, "What is your name?" I said, "My name is Kay Whitaker." In front of all the students, about 90 in the whole class, he asked me to see him after class was over.

This was very scary to me because I thought I had done something wrong and was going to be in deep trouble. He was also a very old and scary-looking professor that everyone made fun of. When students were leaving, I went down front to see him. He came over to me and asked me if I knew Doyle Whitaker and I said, "Yes sir, he is my father." It was there that I reconnected with my dad's geology mentor. Dad was very close to Dr. Jarvis and after his undergraduate studies in geology he got his master's in geology working with Dr. Jarvis the whole time. I suddenly remembered that Mom would tell me that he would come over and eat with her and Dad when Russell and I were little toddlers.

I took two years of geology from Dr. Jarvis before he retired. This professor loved my dad and told me, "I always knew that your dad was going to be one heck of a geologist!" That didn't mean much to me, being a shallow young adult! I had no idea what it took to be great at anything except becoming friends. My time studying geology was amazing and I loved it and made wonderful grades. But as the world dictated, I kept thinking who is going to hire a woman to be a geologist is this day and age? It had to be teaching or nursing. I had my eyes on being a wife of a wonderful Christian guy, and a mother. If I would have been raised in the more liberal world today, my education at TCU would have been as a geology major, like my dad, but women didn't have the choices back then like they have now.

While I was finishing up my first semester, my parents had been getting more involved in some charismatic crowds and learning a great deal about the Holy Spirit. The one church my mom kept mentioning in her letters was The Church of the Redeemer in Houston.

I went with Mom and Dad to one of their weekly evening meetings during freshman Christmas break. I was so moved by the Holy Spirit that I cried. Mom was also involved in some ladies' Bible studies and I could tell she was different. Dad was too. They were members of Tallowood Baptist Church but were out there looking for more of God. They were learning about the Baptism of the Holy Spirit, which I didn't understand and had never heard of. After we came home from The Church of the Redeemer, my mom asked me what I thought about the service, the praise and the worship. I actually told her, "Mom, you know I love the Lord but I don't need Him that much!" How could I say something like that?

So I went back to TCU and I was so glad to be back with Kay and Patti! One Saturday morning, Patti, Kay and I went to IHOP for breakfast. We were sitting in a booth and talking all about the Lord and I'm telling them what happened to me at The Church of the Redeemer. We were talking about wanting more of the Lord, the one thing I denied with my mom. In the booth next to us was a very large man in a suit and his petite wife. As they were leaving, they looked at us and said they heard us talking about the Lord and were so excited that some TCU girls were wanting more of God. They invited us to come to their church the next day.

So off we went to this small Assembly of God Church on the east side of Fort Worth. We were the three TCU girls sitting on the front row like sponges taking it all in. Kenneth Copeland was the speaker. This was his home church before he became famous. There was such a charge in the air, hard to describe but it was the Holy Spirit, alive and well and moving freely. After the sermon they asked if anyone wanted to experience more of the Lord in their life, and without even looking at my friends I stepped forward three steps and hands were laid on me and down I went speaking in tongues, which never happened with the Children of God because there was no Holy Spirit there. I was bawling and praying and praising God. In my whole life I will never forget this experience. It changed my life and I became immersed in the Lord. As I was getting up, I saw Patti and Kay both lying on the floor speaking in tongues too! The Lord zapped all of us together!

This was around the time the Jesus Movement was starting on the TCU campus. Dr. Rex was the man who invited us to come to his church and he introduced the three of us to Orlando and Joanne Reyes, who basically became our mentors for a couple of years and friends for life. Joanne was our Bible study teacher. Patti, Kay and I were enjoying our Bible studies together, and as I look back it is almost like we were in a cocoon during the second semester of freshman year just learning more about God, the Father, Son and Holy Spirit. We were going to downtown Fort Worth with Orlando and witnessing mostly to the homeless on the streets, because that's about all there was in downtown Fort Worth at that time.

Orlando started a coffeehouse called the Cornerstone right on Berry Street next to the railroad tracks. We would go on Saturday nights and invite people on campus to come. Most of the kids on campus were not too responsive, but that was okay because the seeds were being planted. There was great praise and worship and lots of prayer for people who would just walk in off the streets. There was one Hispanic guy named George who came a lot to the Cornerstone and he was an avid witness for the Lord on TCU campus. People started calling him "Hallelujah George" because every time he would see you on campus or anywhere he would just say "Hallelujah!" In the midst of all this activity, I was thriving in my studies. I was enjoying most of my classes, but I switched from history to home economics.

During my sophomore year, I was given the opportunity to go on a European trip for 12 weeks, and at the end of it I could earn 12 hours of credit with a written paper. This was a home economics trip. It included all aspects of home economics in Europe. This was a goldmine of learning and I was so excited. My roommate for the whole trip was a fellow friend from the Pi Phi sorority, Barbara. We went through the whole trip together. In London, we went to all the sights and lectures: Tower of London, William Shakespeare's Stratford on the Avon, the Crown Jewels of London, the Soho district, the British Museum. In France, we took a class at Cordon Bleu cooking school, ate at the top of the Eiffel Tower, Versailles Palace, a Waterford crystal factory, the Louvre Museum and the Mona Lisa along with all the relics from the Assyrian invasion of Israel. My history of the Bible really came to life with what I saw at the Louvre. On to Italy on the train to see the silk farms and Michelangelo's works of art in Florence, including the statue of David and the Sistine Chapel in Rome. We were privileged to see Leonardo da Vinci's "Pieta" and "Moses." I was in such a trance with all of this history that I loved and studied. Then to Rome and seeing the Coliseum where all the Christians were tortured and murdered. Off to Austria and Switzerland where we saw all the beauty that Europe had to offer in 1973. From there we headed to Germany. In the midst of this travel I was reading a new book that had just come out. *The Hiding Place* by Corrie Ten Boom was becoming a best-selling book. This was the true story of a Dutch woman, Corrie Ten Boom, who was the daughter of a clockmaker in Haarlem, Netherlands. This one family made it their mission to rescue and save as many Jewish families from death by the Nazis as they possibly could. I was almost finished reading this book, and I was picturing myself as a victim during this horrific time of history. As our bus would travel through these small villages, I could see through the eyes of Corrie Ten Boom, the Jewish people being rounded up and put on the trains heading to their death. I know that a lot of people never even think of this part of history, but to me I have always been in awe of this story. How could the human race, notably the Germans, go after one race of people and set out to exterminate them within one generation? When I was a young child, my parents had purchased some *Life* magazine books that were all about World War II. I really don't think they intended for their young child to look at them, but I did. There were black and white photos of men, women and children who were the victims of Auschwitz, Bergen Belsen, Dachau and many other locations. I would look at these photos of the emaciated dead in heaps and piles and couldn't imagine any human being doing this to another human being. I was totally captivated that this could happen. Now, years later as a young adult, here I am in the very location where these events actually happened. It saddened me so much that as we would ride the bus through Austria and Germany my roommate would ask me what I was thinking because I was being so quiet, which didn't usually happen. I felt like I was treading on the tombs of the dead. I truly felt like I was walking where the past had walked before. I remember looking out the window of the buses that we travelled in and seeing people in the streets and thinking, "Do they even know or care what happened here in this church square 30 years ago?" I was looking at these sites in 1973 and all these atrocities happened in 1942-1945. At this time there were no tours to the concentration camps and these were not a part of the TCU home economic summer travel abroad program, but I made it mine. Once we reached the end of our journey and I reached the end of *The Hiding Place*, we were in Amsterdam. The tour had given us a great tour of Amsterdam. Visiting Anne Frank's hideout, of which I had read in Anne Frank's diary, was another surreal experience into another human being's life experience. We got to see the art and the other lovely "Red District" sights of Amsterdam.

We were given the following Sunday off and could do whatever we wanted to do. My roomie, Barbara, asked me what I wanted to do and I knew exactly what I wanted to do. I told her that I wanted us to take the train out of Amsterdam to Haarlem. She said, "Why, and where is Haarlem?" I told her that this is where the Ten Boom clock shop was, which meant absolutely nothing to her. Throughout the whole trip since Italy I had been sharing with her information about the Holocaust and she was about 40 percent interested, but this time she was a lot more interested. It was a Sunday morning and we got the train schedule to Haarlem, which was a small village just northwest of Amsterdam. I felt like we were on a big-girl adventure into the past. We kept laughing and saying, "I hope we don't get lost! Do we really know what we are doing?" I never wavered. I truly felt like this was one of the best excursions we were going to have on the whole trip. We got off the train and started walking to the town square where the main cathedral was. Very easy to find. The Ten Boom clock shop was in the southeast corner of the church square. There was no one in the town square and it seemed odd since it was Sunday, but no one was in the church either. Kind of sad for a Sunday. We walked over to the Ten Boom clock shop. It was not open, so we knocked and no one came to answer. I was so sad. We went to the side alley door where the Jews would enter and go into hiding in their upper floors, but no one answered. I just stood there and stared inside and waited. Nothing. But I was here and how blessed was I to be standing where many, many Jews had stood and knocked to be taken in by the Ten Boom family. They were a Christian family who felt the call to save as many Jews as they could from the atrocities of the Germans. They did save many hundreds of Jews from perishing. Eventually, the whole Ten Boom family was rounded up by the Nazis and sent to concentration camps. The only member of Corrie Ten Boom's family who survived the Nazi camps was Corrie. The rest of her family who participated in all these rescues ended up dying in concentration and labor camps.

After we left the clock shop, I told Barbara that I wanted to go to the town square where the cathedral was and where all the Haarlem Jews were rounded up and herded off to the concentration camps. It was there that I really got to feel in a very minuscule way what these wonderful people went through at the hands of an evil, tyrannical and hateful person like Hitler and his whole machine of evil. It was here that I realized that in this world there truly are evil and vile human beings that have as their life goal the destruction of everything good in this life. As you can imagine, this had a huge impact on my life.

CHAPTER 6

TURMOIL IN TEXAS

*Seeing that His divine power has granted to us
everything pertaining to life and godliness, through the true
knowledge of Him who has called us by His own glory
and excellence. For by these He has granted to us His
precious promises, in order that by them you might
become partakers of the divine nature, having escaped the
corruption that is in the world by lust.*

2 PETER 1:3-4

I got home from this great trip and earned my 12 semester hours with my essays. I was ready to start my junior year.

Little did I know that I would meet my best friend forever.

Right around the ending of my sophomore year, a friend of mine, Josh, who was a cheerleader at TCU, told me that his girlfriend from Tennessee was going to be coming to TCU and she was already a Chi Omega from her Tennessee school. He wanted me to be her friend. Sounded good to me. We became such good friends! Our junior year we ended up being roommates in the Chi Omega house. This was when we really got to know each other. I started praying for her and Josh. She saw me study the Bible and she really couldn't wrap her head around that when there was so much partying to be done. Janice and Josh started attending the Campus Crusade for Christ meetings on the campus. There were a lot more people at TCU coming to the Lord by this time. One weekend she asked me to go on a Campus Crusade for Christ retreat with her and Josh. After one of the meetings at the retreat, I went back to our room and didn't know where she was. She came in later, eyes and face red from crying. She gave me a big hug and told me that she and Josh had both accepted the Lord and were truly believers now. She was telling me how grateful she was for my prayers for her and Josh.

One night Janice came home to our room and told me that she and Josh had just met this great guy at a Campus Crusade for Christ meeting. I hadn't dated much my junior year. I had dated a guy my sophomore year, but he was raised a Christian Scientist, and after attending a Christian Scientist service with him I was sure I couldn't do that. So I didn't see that relationship going anywhere from there, plus I wasn't ready for anyone at that point. In the meantime, I had not been around Orlando and Joanne much that past year and Patti had gotten involved with a sect called the Branhamites. Let's just say, I was floundering. There was not a lot of fellowshipping between us. I was kind of in a place where I wasn't sure where I fit in. When they told me about this guy they wanted to introduce me to, I wasn't real keen on meeting him. At this point, I really didn't know what I wanted, except I wanted someone who loved the Lord and loved me. I was still a virgin, saving myself for "the one." Janice told me his name was Steve and he was a student at Southwestern Baptist Seminary and was so cute. She told me that she told him about me and basically set us up. We did go out and went to the park to study together and have picnics. He literally had no money. He was working at night selling cemetery plots for some funeral home. He was very respectful when he would kiss me. He never tried to take it to the next level. I was wanting more, but knew waiting till marriage was the best route. My boyfriend in high school and I fooled around a bit but never went "all the way!" I did get a glimmer of how good this could feel. There was a little chemistry on my part, but he was determined to stay good and not do anything. We dated the rest of that year, and that summer of 1973 we traveled to go meet his family in Paducah, Kentucky. Looking back, there were red flags everywhere. There was a great deal of tension between him and his father. It was so tense I would just sit on the front porch to get away from it. Their lifestyle was so different from how I was raised. I remember how Steve's mom was always trying to fix everything. Make it all okay. The only bright spot in the setting was Steve's younger brother, Paul. He was sweet and so free. He was a contrast to Steve and his sister, Marty, who I didn't meet on this trip but met later. It was like both of them were so ashamed of their family and lifestyle. They couldn't wait to leave and escape to another state. She was a student at Texas Tech. On the road trip home, we had some discussion about family and kids and he told me he would never have children. This was very upsetting to me because I always knew that I did want kids eventually. He never would fully explain to me why he felt this way. Another red flag!

Whenever Steve was around my family, he was very un-comfortable. Mom and Dad later told me that they thought he was a nice, quiet guy. Dad also said he seemed to meet all the criteria: a Christian, going to be in the ministry, good-looking and I seemed happy with him. So many red flags, but we marched forward and got engaged in the fall of 1973 with a wedding planned for March 9, 1974 at Tallowood Baptist Church in Houston.

One fun thing my dad did for me before the wedding was a trip to the Houston Stock Show. He was on the Board and could get really great seats for the shows. He kept it a surprise as to who we were going to see. Every year the Stock Show always had some of the most fabulous entertainers at the Astrodome. When we got to the parking lot I saw the marquee and I screamed! ELVIS PRESLEY! I was so excited and when we got inside our seats were about 20 rows up from the rails around the rodeo arena. The atmosphere was electric, then the music started and in came Elvis sitting on the back of a big white Cadillac, wearing his signature white jumpsuit with gold all over. I was screaming and Dad just nudged me and said, "Why don't you go on down the aisle and get next to the rail before he drives by?" Of course I rocketed down the aisle and when Elvis drove by, I was probably only 15 feet away from him. I was crying and screaming at the same time! I had always been an Elvis fan and so wanted to go to all of his movies, but my mom wasn't too keen on him. She didn't want me to go to the movies, but I did sneak out and see some of them with my friends. When my daughter, Lisa, ended up going to Belmont University in Nashville, I got to go to Graceland a couple of times. The first time was when Christy and I drove with Lisa to settle her into the freshman dorm at Belmont University in Nashville. I told the girls we had to go there when we got to Memphis. I went through the whole home, reading everything and taking it all in. When I got to the tombstones of his parents, his twin brother and Elvis, I saw the girls sitting on a bench. When I walked up and I was so excited about it all, they just said "We don't get it!" It was a truly emotional experience for me, for I truly believed that Elvis was a wonderful person and because he was so good at what he did, he was taken advantage of by many people.

Meanwhile back to the Houston Astrodome 1974. After Elvis passed by, I ran back to my seat and was still crying and couldn't believe I got to see Elvis in person. I told Dad I couldn't help but cry and scream. He said, "Hey man, I almost started crying too!"

The wedding day came. It was a big blowout wedding and reception. No holds barred! Looking back, I remember that all of Steve's buddies from Campus Crusade were his grooms-men. I really never met any of them. I wish I would have spent some time with them. Maybe I could have gotten more insight into who he was. I do remember that among these guys they talked about a guy named Duke, who sounded like he was some kind of mentor to them. Steve never would clarify. Mom told me after I had moved back to Houston two years later that at the wedding when the mothers were lining up to walk down the aisle, Steve's mom came up to her and said, "Oh Marjorie, I hope Kay can help Steve!" Mom told me that at that moment she should have cancelled everything. But we went on. After the wedding, we spent our first night together in a hotel near my parents' home and then the next day we were driving back to Fort Worth to set up our home. That first night was very awkward and unsatisfying to say the least. I was sad.

When we got back to Fort Worth, we were in the married housing for the seminary students at Southwestern Seminary and met another really nice couple, Marty and Jan Brown. What a contrast I got to see. They were very affectionate and fun in contrast to our seriousness and no chemistry or affection. In fact, Steve even stopped talking to me like he did when we were dating. He was rarely home. I spent many hours alone. He worked late into the night. We struggled financially, and of course my Grandma Whitaker knew this so she would send me all her S&H green stamps with books. I would put them all in the books and save enough to walk to the S&H stamp store close by on Seminary South Drive. She was always so thoughtful and it was such a treat for me to go shopping without spending any money! Our sex life was strange to say the least. Not that I was an expert in lovemaking but I just thought there should be more romance and fun leading up to the whole thing. It was quick and done. I really didn't know who I could talk to about it, but I would always think of Marty and Jan, who had this chemistry. I was looking for help, but I was too embarrassed to ask her about it or share what I was feeling with anyone. I heard about two books that would help women woo their men and improve their sex lives. One was *Fascinating Womanhood* and the other by Marabel Morgan was called *The Total Woman*. I tried a few of the antics in these books and nothing seemed to change. So I basically just gave up and stayed as busy as I could.

We would go to Throckmorton when Mom and Dad came up from Houston to visit. Steve would always find projects for himself to do so he wouldn't have to sit around on the breezeway and visit, which is what we would always do. My dad bought him a Stetson hat our first Christmas. He would always wear it when we went to Throckmorton. Looking back, it was pretty pathetic that a non-Texan could ever fake being a Texan with a Stetson hat on. It just didn't work.

One particular time, he wanted to paint the rusty metal cattle corral that was out at the Buchanan place. It was some acreage my granddad had southeast of Throckmorton. Granddad was like "Sure, go for it" while scratching his head in puzzlement. It was probably 110 degrees outside. Off Steve went to get the paint and supplies. With his cowboy hat on, he headed out and got to painting. He did this for two solid days and finished right about the time we had to leave to go back to Fort Worth. While he was not around us, my parents told me how strange they thought this was. They were pretty sure he did not like his new in-laws. I couldn't disagree. Who would spend all day under the hot sun out in the country painting an old rusted corral? To this day, 35 years later, when we drive to Throckmorton and pass by the Buchanan place, there is still that old, now faded, red corral.

I was still planning to graduate from TCU, but I was going to finish my last semester in the fall of 1974. In the meantime, I did volunteer work at Fort Worth Children's Hospital and I really enjoyed that. My parents would come up and visit me, but Steve was never around. I actually started taking piano lessons again during the spring semester after getting married. At the end of the semester, I was going to play in a piano recital. My parents and my maternal grandmother came to the recital, but no Steve. He had become a permanent no-show in my life.

After I graduated in winter 1974, Steve got a weekend job being the youth director at Trinity Baptist Church in Kerrville, Texas. So every weekend from Friday until Sunday night, we were gone to Kerrville. It was about a five-hour drive from Fort Worth. The people in this small church were so kind to us. I got close to two of the deacons' wives, Sue and Joy. They were in their early 40s and kind of took me under their wings. We would stay in people's homes on the weekends.

After he graduated from seminary, Trinity offered Steve a full-time job as the Youth Director. We moved to Kerrville in the summer of 1975 after he graduated. The first place we lived was a rental house that a member of the church owned. It was perched high above Kerrville with great views of the sleepy little town and the Guadalupe River rolling through the middle of town. I thought Kerrville was beautiful. I was alone a lot. Steve was at the church all the time. I was about three months pregnant at this point. There was absolutely no sex anymore, because when I announced to him back in April 1975 that I was pregnant, he actually told me, "There is no way I could have sex with a pregnant woman. It would be gross!" When I think back on that time, I really had no one to con-fide in, being the youth pastor's wife. I didn't know how to process any of what was going on between us. I really didn't have anything to compare this life with, but in my imagination I thought it should have been so much better. I was so happy to be pregnant. He kept announcing to everyone at the church that he was going to have a son, and I would tell him that we don't know what the sex of this baby is so be careful, it could be a girl. He would have none of that talk. It was just me and the Lord most days. In the fall, we moved into a rent house closer to the church.

My parents knew things were weird, but not knowing what to say, they said nothing. Later my parents told me they just thought he hated them. No one in our family had ever gotten a divorce, so they never went there.

During the Christmas of 1975, I was eight months pregnant and the doctor didn't want me to travel. Dad rented a condo at River Hill Country Club in Kerrville. My mom, dad, sister, brother and my mom's parents all came and stayed in the condo while Steve and I were able to stay at our house. We had our Christmas celebration there with Mom cooking wonderful meals. It was an awkward time because Steve was definitely a no-show every day they were there. However, on Christmas Day he did show up for that celebration. My parents said nothing about the strained atmosphere, but all of us could feel it.

It was during these last few months of my pregnancy that I was reading the book *Christy* by Catherine Marshall. I had read another of her books and liked her stories and writing a lot. This was a biography of her grandmother, who was a young teacher to the illiterate children in the mountains of Tennessee back in the early 1900s. As I was reading this inspiring story, I kept thinking to myself that the child I was carrying was very special to me, being my firstborn. I couldn't quit sensing that this baby was a girl, despite all that Steve was saying about having a son. While reading this book, I decided that this baby girl was going to be called Christy, Christy Kay.

As I got closer to the delivery date, my mother said that she would come after the baby was born and take care of us. I was on board with that. I was due around January 18, 1976. Close to my due date, I started walking every day, like my friend Joy told me to do so it would help induce labor.

On January 12, I went into labor after my walk and my water broke. Steve was home at the time and he took me to the hospital in downtown Kerrville. This was in the day when no one went into the labor room, not even the husband. You were with the doctor and the nurse and the husband sat (or paced) out in the waiting room. Around midnight on January 13, Christy Kay was born and yes, she was a girl. The doctor went out and told Steve that he had healthy baby girl. He never came up to see me after that. He went home. I thought that was weird! I called my mom and dad from the hospital and gave them the good news about their firstborn granddaughter. Since I had a spinal for labor pain, they told me I would be in the hospital for at least two days. Mom and Dad said they would be there in a day or two. The first morning after Christy was born, the nurse brought her in to me and I nursed her. No Steve. The nurse did tell me that I had a guest. Joy was there. I was so glad to see her, but when she came into my room I could tell that she was angry. I asked her what was going on and she asked me, "What IS going on?" I didn't understand. She said, "What is wrong with your husband?" I didn't know what to say so I cried! She hugged me and said, "This is just postpartum hormones." Then she told me that she had gone by the church that morning and saw Steve. He said nothing about Christy being born. Then she went to Mr. Beach's pharmacy across the street from the hospital and a nurse was there visiting with Mr. Beach, who was a deacon in our church. The nurse had told Mr. Beach that the youth director's wife had a baby girl last night and was still in the hospital. So she came over to see me and find out why Steve had not shared any of this with the people at the church. I just kept crying because I didn't know what to tell her. She left me and said she was going to confront Steve. Right after she left, my parents walked in the door and held little Christy in their arms. Of course Dad was asking, "Where the heck is Steve?" "I guess he is at work." My dad was not satisfied with that answer. That day, I got discharged from the hospital, so my dad called the church and spoke to Steve, "Kay is clear to come home and she's ready for you to come pick her and Christy up." He just casually asked Dad if he would bring me and Christy home since he was already up there. My dad's face got so red and he said, "She is your wife and your baby! You get your butt up here right now!" I started crying again. Steve reluctantly came and took me and Christy home. Mom said she would stay with me, so Dad left to go back to Houston. While she was there, Steve never came to the house during the day. He never held Christy. He showed up very late at night after Mom had gone to bed and left before anyone got up. After one day at the house with me and Christy, my mom called Dad. She wanted him to come and take her back to Houston. She told me the atmosphere and the tension in the house was more than she could stand. After she left, I was alone again, except this time I had my baby girl to take care of. Steve would come in and out and not even acknowledge that there was a new little life in the back bedroom. A couple of nights after Mom left, Steve came in very late acting very edgy and nervous. It was scaring me. I was in bed reading when he came in. Christy was asleep in her crib in the next room. He started pacing back and forth at the foot of the bed, grabbing his head.

He kept saying, "I'm going crazy, I don't know what's wrong with me!" He kept pacing and raging. I was crying out of fear and saying, "Let's go see a counselor, we need to get some help." He abruptly stopped and looked at me and said he needed to hold his baby. I immediately jumped out of bed and ran to Christy's crib and picked her up before he got into her room. When I went back to bed with her I saw that he was gone. I had never been terrorized before, but that night I was.

I kept Christy in bed with me until the sun came up. No Steve. As soon as the sun was up, I wanted to call my dad but not at the house because I was afraid Steve would come home. So I got Christy and drove to the town square next to the courthouse where there was a payphone booth. I shared with my dad everything that happened last night. He had a plan. He told me exactly what to do and who to confide in. So I called Sue, whom I really liked. She was a deacon's wife whom I had gotten close to. I started packing a bag and got all my baby items in another bag. I wrote Steve a letter to tell him what I was doing, where I was going and that I wanted him to get some help. As I looked around our little rent house, I saw all the wedding gifts that mostly my friends and family gave us and just let it all go. I had to protect myself and my new baby.

Sue and Ben came to pick us up and took us to the San Antonio airport. Ben drove my car and Christy and I were in Sue's car. On the drive to San Antonio, I told her all that had happened. She started sharing with me some of the antics that

Steve had been doing at the church, of which I had no idea. Steve had several incidents where he would get angry with some of the youth and take them into the bathroom, shove their heads into the toilet while he flushed it. I was shocked. Apparently the whole church was in turmoil over Steve and the pastor was about to be fired too. Youth pastor's wife is always the last to know.

CHAPTER 7

HAVOC IN HOUSTON

Weeping may endure for the night,
but a shout of joy comes in the morning.
PSALM 30:5

I believe that I will see the goodness
of the Lord in the land of the living.
PSALM 27:13

Once we got to the airport, Mom, Christy and I got on the
plane back to Houston and Dad drove my car to Houston.

When we got to my parent's home in Houston that night, I
got a call from Sue and she was in shock. She said that she had
gone by our house to see if Steve was there. He was gone. He
had cleared out the whole house and she said there was nothing left in the house. It was totally empty. Steve had packed it
all and took off. He didn't even tell the church. He just left and
she had no idea where he went, and of course I didn't either. I
couldn't imagine how he got all our stuff out of the house and

left Kerrville in such a hurry. I never did find out. For about two weeks I had no idea where he went or what he was doing or thinking.

Being with Mom and Dad during this phase was really healing because I told them all that had happened and how odd life was with him. Mom and I talked about our sex life or lack thereof. I shared with her some things that had occurred and she would just keep saying, "This is not normal!" One day I got a package in the mail from Steve with a note. It was some of my lingerie that I received at a bridal shower. The note just said, "Just seeing and feeling your lingerie makes me want you." My mom freaked out. With all that was going on, this was outrageous! Some nights I would hear a pebble hit my upstairs window at my parents' home and it would be Steve standing down in the front yard. He would drive in the night to show up between two and four in the morning. It just got stranger too.

In the meantime, Mom and I were taking care of Christy. I was having a horrible time trying to nurse her with all the tension around us. Mom said what I needed was a beer or wine to help me relax and nurse better. I never drank, so this was a new activity. Mom bought a bottle of Blue Nun wine and some Heineken beer. I would drink a beer before feeding Christy. It did help me relax, but after about two weeks I realized this dream of nursing my baby wouldn't come true. So we started her on formula. She started spitting it up in a large way. We told the doctor, so she started her on a soy formula. She suspected Christy was allergic to cow's milk. This helped and she continued to grow and thrive. I was getting stronger and recovering from childbirth.

I reached out to Steve's mom, Eunice, and told her that we would love for her to come to Houston to see Christy, her first grandchild. We offered to fly her down. She refused but was very grateful for the offer. She never asked about Steve. I wasn't sure what she knew and if she had even spoken to him. Little did she know that it would be 24 years later that she would meet her first granddaughter.

One day, my friend Janice from TCU called and said she had heard that I had moved back to Houston and split with Steve. That is all she knew. I had never shared with her all the drama about Steve. Janice and Josh had gotten married in 1973. I was maid of honor at their wedding in Tennessee. She was really busy finishing at TCU after that. Josh had a job selling houses in Dallas. We had lost touch when they moved to Dallas. I didn't want to share how bad my marriage to Steve was because I was ashamed. She said she wanted to come and visit me at my parents' home. I said okay. She had her firstborn daughter about a month before Christy was born. Her name was Ashley and she was a preemie. When Janice came down, we laid the girls down next to each other and Christy was twice as big as little Ashley. It was a very awkward visit because sharing with her what had transpired was really hard. As the afternoon wore on, I could see what her motive was for coming down. She believed I was disobeying the Lord and needed to restore the relationship and return to Steve. I couldn't make her understand what was going on. She kept going on, and of course I started crying because I felt condemned and there didn't seem to be any attempt to understand. My dad could hear what was going on upstairs and he marched up the stairs and told her she needed to leave.

He told her that if she couldn't come and visit without such a condemning attitude he would rather she leave. Of course, she left after that and we didn't reconnect for 25 years. Later, when we did reconcile, we definitely made up for the lost years.

Steve would make odd appearances, wanting to see Christy. We would let him come in and Dad would follow him upstairs where her crib and a rocking chair was. I was usually in the backyard or gone.

He finally told me that he was in Fort Worth living with a couple we both had met at Birchman Avenue Baptist Church several years back. I asked him about our stuff and he said it was in a storage unit in Fort Worth. I told him that my mom and I wanted to go to it and get some of our family items. He agreed, so Mom and I drove up there. His friend met us and opened the unit. I got all of my grandmother's homemade quilts and china that I had selected. I got things that I couldn't replace. Family heirlooms. But there was so much that I would never lay eyes on again. It was just stuff!

As I got stronger, I wanted to start working as a substitute teacher at my old high school. Dad wanted me to have space of my own so he bought a small condo about a 10-minute drive from their house.

Finally, we realized that divorce was inevitable. So we hired an attorney, Dan Brown. He said that in Harris County I couldn't file for divorce until I had lived there for six months. This was in March, so we realized that it would not happen until June. So life went on. I would work substituting and Mom was watching Christy. We all started attending Evangelistic Temple in Houston. Mom, Dad and I were really heavy into the charismatic movement and ET was a hub for great teaching. While attending, I found out they had a singles group, but there was no way I was going to attend. I was not even divorced yet. I had filed for divorce in February of 1976 and had to wait for six months for it to be final. Steve was served with the papers, but he never said anything to me about it. No arguing, no asking me to come back, nothing. It was so odd.

During this time my cousin, who lived in Arlington, called me to tell me that her other cousin had seen Steve in a singles group at her church. She said that he was in the small group and they were sharing about themselves. When it came to him, he shared that he had never been married and he had no children. Of course Erin knew who he was and that all he shared was a lie. I guess he was trying to start a new life for himself in Fort Worth as a single.

Summer of 1976 was going well. Divorce was hard, but it was final in July of 1976. Steve's visitation guidelines were to see Christy at my parents' home every other Sunday. He didn't come for all his visits, just sporadically. When he did come, he would go upstairs to her room and spend time with her while my dad was upstairs in another room. I was never there when he came. I had moved to a condo. Steve never knew about that.

I started attending the singles group at ET after the divorce was final. I was making some really nice friends, and to this day I am close friends with my favorite, Pat. She married the head of the singles group, Charles. I continued to visit and noticed the worship leader every Sunday, John Apple. He started to pursue me. I was really impressed with his leadership on the worship team. We started dating on a slow basis and did a lot of double-dating with Pat and Charles. Those were fun, free-spirited days. We went to Galveston together, went out for dinner and played tennis. John worked as an expeditor for Brown and Root company out of Houston. He had a regular job and loved the Lord. He was very outgoing, funny and charismatic. I was looking for anyone not like Steve. Our relationship grew quickly. I was getting more enamored with him every day. He was very affectionate and touchy-feely. I loved this because I was starved for it. Someone who liked me just for who I was and didn't ignore me. I met John's mom, Olive, early on and really liked her. She was divorced from John's dad and worked as a PE teacher in a Pasadena high school. I never met his dad until after we married. John never wanted to talk about him, but I learned from his mom that his alcoholism is why they split up and it was still bad at the time. Later I found out that his dad was living with his own elderly mother and could hardly take care of himself.

While at Evangelistic Temple, I was seeing a counselor to deal with the ups and downs from my divorce with Steve. The more I told him about Steve during our marriage and his behavior now, the more concerned he was getting. He was worried that Steve might try to take Christy if he had the opportunity. So he advised me to tell the nursery workers at church to only allow me, my parents or John to pick her up. She was only seven months old at this time. John and I were still just dating. When I told the sweet nursery ladies who the only people were that could pick Christy up, you could see in their faces that they were already nervous.

In the meantime, fall rolled around and I started substitute teaching at my old high school. Mom thought it was time to try and hire a nanny for Christy. We interviewed the first lady who came to the house, Ruthie Horne. She showed up on time at my parents' house in her crisp white uniform. She was very sweet, outgoing and praising the Lord. We immediately thought we should give her a try. Her only job was babysitting Christy at my parents' house when I was at work. She didn't do any housework because we had Priscilla, who had been doing that for my mom for years. So Ruthie was now a part of our household.

John and I were getting seriously involved from August to September. He was very persuasive to me and very outgoing around my family. He was also funny and had inherited the salesmanship gene from his car-selling dad back in the day at Osborne Apple Ford Company in Pasadena, Texas. I was very drawn to his charisma and passion. This certainly didn't feel mysterious like it did with Steve. He was a joy with his guitar playing and leading worship in the singles group. What girl in that group wouldn't want to go out with him! I did go out with another guy in that group once and I just thought he was boring. We were getting close really fast. Too fast for my parents. They were getting nervous at the pace and told me I should slow things down. I was happy and liked the way things were going.

We were still having issues with Steve and visitation. It was sporadic and uneventful. A couple of Sundays after my last visit to the counselor, I was sitting in the sanctuary and I just happened to turn around. I saw Steve glaring at me from the back of the church.

I was so scared because the look was piercing. I was at the front of the church, so I immediately exited out the front side entrance. I went to the nursery to pick up Christy. The lady grabbed my arm at the nursery door and said that a man, who said he was Christy's dad, tried to get her. She said that they told him he wasn't on the list of people who could pick her up. She also said he was very angry when they wouldn't let him pick her up.

This particular weekend was his weekend to see her but he was so sporadic I wasn't keeping up. I grabbed Christy and put her in my car and started heading to Mom and Dad's house. It was raining a "Houston" rainstorm. It was so bad that I couldn't see the car in front of me. I would stop under bridges hoping it would let up. If you've ever lived in Houston, you totally know what I am talking about. I was so nervous and scared thinking that Steve might be right behind me in this awful rainstorm. I finally made it to Mom and Dad's. Once I got there I saw that John had come over from church too. After I explained what had happened in the church and the nursery, the doorbell rang. My heart was racing and I was getting nauseated. Dad answered and it was Steve. Dad acted surprised to see Steve and asked him what he could do for him. Steve announced, "I'm here to pick Christy up and take her to the Houston Museum of Art." I was frantic. I just started shouting at him, "There is no way you are taking this seven-month-old baby to a museum in this weather or any weather. The nerve you have trying to take her out of the nursery without asking me!" Emotions were running high and Dad tried to calm everyone down. Mom took Christy upstairs. John charged at Steve. I was so afraid someone was going to get hurt. Dad got between them and told Steve to leave. Steve threatened all of us with arrest if anything like this ever happened again. Thankfully, he finally left.

The next day Mom shared with Ruthie all that had transpired on Sunday. She told her to be very careful who she talked to and not to ever let Steve come into the house. She was very sympathetic with us about all that happened. The next couple of days we started getting these weird threatening phone calls about someone hurting me and Christy.

We were getting really paranoid now. My dad didn't even want me going to work anymore. A few days later, Ruthie came to work and she was shaking. She told us that someone had accosted her with a gun when she got off her bus. He told her he would kill her. She lived on the east side of downtown Houston in a bad crime area and rode a bus all the way to the west side of Houston, in the Memorial area, to work for us.

The nightmare started from there. The calls continued and if we didn't answer, the answering machine took the call. The voice on the other end was gravelly and evil sounding. The threats were to kill me and Christy. This person always would know where I had been. We thought it must be Steve lurking around to know where I was and where Christy was. He had some friends from seminary in the area, so we thought maybe he was staying with them and they were helping him do this to us. At this point my dad decided to hire a private investigator to see what was going on.

We hired John Craig, PI, to help us figure all this out and who was responsible. Try to remember who all is involved in this scenario. My parents had let me come home to live with them while I figured things out, but I still had a sister who at this time was a senior in high school. There were a lot of dynamics going on and a lot of fear.

The PI, John Craig, checked out the seminary friends of Steve and one of them was eventually charged with aggravated assault against Ruthie at the bus stop and he confessed. He did say that he was part of a homosexual group in the area. Yes, he did know Steve Miles. To this day, I really don't understand how any of this was connected. After John and I married in October 1976, we lived in the condo. We started having some issues with my "submission." One day he actually threatened to "spank" me because I didn't agree with him on something. I was appalled and I actually laughed because I thought he was kidding. Since we were still going to Evangelistic Temple, I made an appointment with the counselor I had seen earlier, who warned us that Steve might try to take Christy out of the nursery. We went several times and it was definitely clear that a husband has no right or reason to "spank" his wife. The underlying control issues were never discussed, though, because I really didn't know at this point how bad they would become. During all this commotion, John became very ill with ulcerative colitis. He had to go to the hospital. We were in the middle of this scary campaign and didn't know what to do. So one Saturday morning, baby Christy, Dad, Mom and I headed off to see John in the hospital. Dad brought his gun with us whenever we needed to go anywhere now. Because of his extreme abdominal pain, John stayed in the hospital for a few days to get relief from the colitis. John's mother called my mom and she was angry that he was in the hospital and not working. She basically told my mom to tell John to get up and go back to work. I didn't really understand at the time why she was being so harsh.

When you get married to someone so quickly, there are many surprises that pop up after the "I dos." We were having a few of those! We started heading to the hospital when Mom realized that John didn't have any pajamas. She wanted us to stop at Bilao's and get a pair. The store was not opened yet. My dad was very paranoid being out like this and he had his shotgun right next to him. When we turned into the deserted parking lot, a car followed us and parked behind us. Dad moved very quickly and jumped out of the car, pointing his gun at the man. He quickly left. We were so scared and drove off like lightning. Fortunately, when we left the lot, we ended up at a small village police station. Dad went in and told them what had happened, but there was nothing they could do because we never got the license plate number.

The next move was that PI, John Craig, said that he was going to set up a spying operation in Fort Worth where Steve had an apartment. He thought that he could figure out if Steve was involved in the Houston incidents.

From his sightings, he relayed that Steve and other male companions in bathrobes were a part of his parties he had at the apartment. John Craig and his wife said they would see males of varying ages coming and going from his apartment.

This was very disconcerting to me because it confirmed to me that he was probably bisexual and might be a part of a ring that was trying to scare us and make us afraid that he was going to hurt me or Christy.

When John Craig came on board, he interviewed all of us separately to try and figure out what was going on. When he couldn't figure anything out he got a subpoena to have all the phone lines bugged without any of us knowing, even at my condo.

John Craig had set up a sting operation to uncover the person he believed was responsible for all the fear and confusion surrounding Christy and me. John and I had married on October 10, 1976 in Houston in the midst of all this craziness. Shortly after this, John Craig told John that he should take me and Christy to Throckmorton because it was getting dangerous. My little sister, Cheryl, was told to go stay with her girlfriends and my mom and dad were supposedly going to "take a trip" and leave Ruthie at the house to babysit the house. John Craig had all he needed on tape. He had only shared with my dad that the culprit was Ruthie, our nanny. He was going to set Ruthie up while we were all gone so he could get Ruthie arrested. He had tapes of her from her home threatening and deceiving us. He also had tapes of her in a very evil gruff voice calling her own girls and telling them to go out and pimp for her. She required her girls to prostitute themselves and bring in so much money a day for her. After it was all over, we would listen to the tapes of her talking to her girls and her husband about getting out there and pimping for her. It was disgusting and unbelievable that a mother could do that. Ruthie would speak in the most foul language I have ever heard a woman use. What a contrast to the crispy white uniform and praising-the-Lord nanny that we hired. She truly was a wolf in sheep's clothing.

Years later, Mom told me some stories of how wicked and mean Ruthie was. One day while she was at the house alone with Christy, she called CPS and reported that we were abusing Christy because of the alleged bruises on her. She was at Mom's house when she made the call. A few days later, Mom had come home to find a strange car parked in front. She introduced herself and told Mom there had been an anonymous abuse report and she needed to see the baby and check her for bruises. Mom let this lady in to inspect Christy. She found that all was well. All the while, Ruthie was watching this. Mom told Ruthie that she believed it was Steve who made the call. Another day, a hearse shows up in front of the house and the man comes to the door and states, "I am here to pick up the body." And Mom said, "What body?" The man said, "It's Kay or Doyle Whitaker." Of course my mom was so upset. There were many other calls that Craig had recorded on our home phone. We listened to all of the tapes after she got arrested. She had a very sick mind. John had the setup ready. Ruthie was alone at my parents' house. It was dark and John knocked on the door. He got behind the big tree next to the front porch. She answered and she knew that it was him standing behind the big tree to the right of the front door. Ruthie called out, "Mr. Craig, where are you? I can't see you." John Craig sees Ruthie's gun and tells her, "Ruthie, drop the gun, the police are on their way. It's over!" She did what he said and he got her gun. The police arrived and arrested her and hauled her off to jail.

John Craig came over to my parents' house the next day and let them listen to her on the phone tapes. Mom called me at my grandparents' and told us what had happened. We were shocked, especially when they played the tape of Ruthie's cruel voice and making all the threats she did to us and to her own girls. How did we get so deceived by her? Was any of this from Steve or was he totally innocent? John Craig did think that he was involved in some of the homosexual activity, but for sure he knew the threats were all Ruthie Horne. He thought eventually she was going to start asking for money from Dad or else we would be harmed. Prayer during all this was the Rock in all this turmoil.

After life settled down, we came back to Houston. Steve never came around anymore to see Christy, so I was going to seek to terminate his parental rights. We proceeded with our attorney, Dan Brown. He sent out subpoenas to Steve in Fort Worth to appear two months later for the hearing to terminate. Two months came and went. We were sitting in the judge's chamber waiting for more than an hour. Steve never showed up. The judge said that he had plenty of time to show up. She declared that his parental rights were terminated due to default. He was a no-show. John and I were planning on John adopting her and giving her his name. This would eventually happen in Breckenridge, Texas, where we moved in January of 1977.

Around February, I get a call from Dan Brown, our former attorney, and he told me the oddest story. He said he was in the lobby of one of the courtrooms in downtown Houston and saw this guy wandering around. He asked if he could help him and asked his name. He told him his name and immediately Dan recognized him. He said that Steve was carrying a big red notebook entitled "Bill Gothard Family Basic Institute Studies." Steve told him that he was there for his parental rights hearing involving Christy. Dan told him that the hearing was in January and that he was served with papers two months prior to that. He told him his parental rights were terminated due to him being a no-show. Steve left the courthouse. I didn't hear from him again for several years.

CHAPTER 8

SIDETRACKED IN ABILENE

The battle is not yours but God's.
2 CHRONICLES 20:15

The Lord is the Defense of my life, whom shall I dread?
PSALM 27:1

We moved from Houston to Breckenridge, Texas in 1977. My parents were planning on leaving Houston when my sister graduated from high school that May. In the summer of 1977 they moved to a house they bought in Breckenridge. John and I were in a small apartment in Breckenridge. While we were in Breckenridge, John's adoption of Christy took place and her name was changed to Christy Kay Apple. John and I were having some issues with his impatience and cruelty to Christy. I couldn't stand it, but by that time I was afraid of his temper. One night on a trip from Houston to Breckenridge, we stopped to have dinner in a small town off Highway 6. Christy was only 14 months old and was fussy. She wouldn't eat. John made a big scene and tried to force her to eat. She started crying and people all around were watching us. I confronted him and told him to quit. He wasn't going to have any part of that. He got up abruptly and just said, "Fine, I'll just start walking back to Houston!" I sat there after he left, trying to calm Christy down, and then went to get in the car. I had the keys to the car and I could see his body walking south down the highway on the side of the road. I remember thinking, "Do I go get him and give in to this or keep heading north to Breckenridge, while he heads to Houston?" If I had known what I learned later, I would have made a totally different decision. I should have headed north and not given in to his temper tantrums. Instead, I headed south and picked him up. I apologized and of course he knew he had won. He got in the car and we headed north to home. This became a pattern for me until years later when I started going to counseling and getting help on changing the dynamics of this dysfunctional relationship. Incidents like this were fairly common, but as in any dysfunctional pattern like this, the making up was as good as the bad relating was. So there was a lot of making up. The person who suffered from this was my little 14-month-old, whom John had sworn to protect and take care of as he stood before the judge to adopt her. When we lived in Breckenridge, we would go to Throckmorton and visit my grandparents. Breckenridge was only about 45 minutes south of Throckmorton. By this time my parents had moved from Houston to Breckenridge and were settled there. I loved going to see my grandparents in Throckmorton. We were all together and loved the fact that we saw each other on a regular basis, which was so odd for this clan. Granddad adored Christy. One morning in 1978, they dropped by Mom and Dad's place in Breckenridge and Christy and I were there. They were on their way south to Gatesville, where Granddad would get his pernicious anemia shots. They had just bought a brand-new four-door Lincoln Continental. Their terrier, Fritz, was sitting right between them in the front seat. After some kisses and hugs, off they went. It was several hours later and my dad called me, crying. He told me that Granddad and Grandma had been in a terrible car accident in Gatesville, Texas.

They had been struck from the back of Granddad's side of the car by a big water truck running a red light. My granddad was crushed and died instantly. Fritz was thrown out the front window and died. Thank God, my grandma wasn't thrown out, but she had some not too serious injuries. This devastated my dad and all of us. I was so grateful that we still had Grandma, but she was devastated because Granddad had always been her strength and guide, with her blindness. Needless to say, this was a very sad time for our family.

Later that summer we moved to Abilene, about 45 minutes west. John wanted to pursue a degree at Hardin Simmons University in business and finance. My dad was all for it and wanted to help him with school. We lived in a little rent house close to downtown Abilene. Later we bought a house with a down payment my granddad had given me two years before. At this time, I was substitute teaching again and was in line to get a full-time home economics job to replace the current pregnant home economics teacher. This was at Madison Jr. High for ninth grade. We were also getting involved at First Baptist Church in the young marrieds group.

In the summer of 1978, I found out I was pregnant. I was due in January of 1979. Lisa Jeannette Apple was born January 18, 1979. Prior to her birth, my parents were so excited to live close to us when we had Lisa. They would talk about the birth and predicted that the baby would be a redhead like my dad. Mom said she always wanted a redhead. They would go a step further and tease that if the baby were a redhead we would call her or him "Red Apple!"

All went well with the pregnancy and her birth. John was so excited to have a redheaded baby girl and of course my parents were ecstatic. Such a stark difference from my first delivery. To have a joyous occasion with the birth of my second child was a wonderful contrast to the birth of my first. Unfortunately, this did not last long. Mom came and stayed with us postpartum and things were not all rosy. Mom shared with me about some actions John took with Christy that really upset her during the time she was at our home. She said that one day she realized how mean John was to Christy. I had seen it at times but not to this extreme. Christy, who was three at the time, had asked John for an ice cream cone. He brought her a bowl of ice cream. She said, "I don't want this, I want a cone." Instead of a calm and patient parental response, Mom saw John push her head into the bowl of ice cream. Mom yelled at John and said, "John, I heard you swear to God that you would take care of her. What is this?" She called Dad who drove the 40 minutes from Breckenridge to Abilene. There was a lot of drama and tears. They stayed in a hotel there in Abilene where Mom said she cried all night long thinking about John's abuse of Christy. The next morning they came and John was threatening to quit school. Dad calmed him down and encouraged him to stay in school. John won that round with his threats.

John was getting a job after he got out of school with a real estate company in Abilene, but he had to go to some school in San Antonio for a commercial real estate license. He called me from a San Antonio hospital and said he was extremely ill with meningitis. I went down to see him. I brought him back to Abilene and he was in the hospital for a few days and was not a very compliant patient. I remember the doctor telling him, "I'm going to throw you out this window if you don't do what I'm telling you to do!" What the doctor didn't know: No one could tell John what to do.

Life was not getting any better in Abilene, plus John had made some enemies there. My mom and one of her minister friends, Marianne Sitton, came over to pray for us without Dad. Marianne said that she sensed that we needed to be in a place where we could get better biblical teaching and encouragement. John mentioned that he wanted to move to the Dallas/Fort Worth area. So we left Abilene, much to my dad's disapproval, and started over.

CHAPTER 9

LIFE IN PLANO

The Lord is righteous in all His ways, and kind in all His
deeds. The Lord is near to all who call upon Him, to all who
call upon Him in truth. He will fulfill the desire of those who
fear Him. The Lord keeps all who love Him. He will also hear
their cry and will save them.

PSALM 145:17-19

In late 1980, we moved into an apartment in Euless, Texas because we thought this would give us a halfway point between Fort Worth and Dallas. We weren't exactly sure where we wanted to end up living. When we got an apartment, we set up our phone service and we both decided that we could probably not get another unlisted number here because Steve would not know where we were. I was not sure where he was at this point. Not long after we got our phone and listed phone number our phone rang at two in the morning. I picked it up and on the other end I heard a very gruff, scary-sounding voice saying, "I know where you are." I hung up. I was terrorized and panicking. I told John, "I know that was Steve! We have to get an unlisted number!" I called my mom the next day to tell her what had happened and she said that the day before she had talked to her mom, my maternal grandmother, who lived in Handley close to Fort Worth. She said that my grandfather, Luther, had run into Steve at the Piggly Wiggly on Meadowbrook Drive. He said Steve was very friendly and started inquiring about me and Christy. Of course, my grandfather was not aware of all that had transpired in Houston, so he told Steve that we were in the Metroplex and lived in Euless. So there you go, that's how he knew to look up our number. It was surreal. From then on, we always had an unlisted phone number.

We left Euless and moved to Plano. We ended up attending a charismatic church in Plano we had heard about called Fountain Gate Church. We bought a home close to the church. It was a vibrant and very exciting worship experience and there was great Bible teaching. Fuchsia Pickett and Judson Cornwall were the primary teachers there. There was an academy, where Christy eventually went to kindergarten and first grade. There was also a Bible college, where I took some great classes.

This was in summer of 1981. We made lots of new friends here and John got a job with a group of guys in the church who were part of an oil exploration and investment company. Life was good in the beginning. There were still the incidents that I pretty much overlooked.

John was beginning to not like the fact that I was spending a lot of time with my new friends while he was at work. Now that he was working, he had less control over me. He would sometimes make negative comments about some of my friends, trying to keep me from seeing them. There were times when I would go to lunch with my friend Dena. I would share with her how he was trying to keep me isolated. She told me that some of our friends could see the way John treated me when we would all get together. She said it made them uncomfortable.

As we kept talking and sharing, she suggested I try Al-Anon. She knew John was not an alcoholic, but she thought the support and sharing would help me somehow.

One week later, I went to my first Al-Anon meeting really close to my house. Everyone was very welcoming to me since I was the "newbie." At Al-Anon, they go around the table and share what the daily devotional had meant to them and relate it to their life. I can't remember what the devotional theme was for that day, but I do remember crying while they all recited the "Serenity Prayer" at the very beginning of the meeting. After that, the sharing started if anyone wanted to. I stayed weepy the whole time they all shared. I listened to these people sharing about their husbands, wives or children, who are alcoholics, and how they are using the 12 steps to cope with their scenarios. I kept thinking that I don't live with a person who drinks any alcohol. I was getting confused and upset. By the time it came time for me to share, I was still crying. When they asked if I wanted to share I said, "Sure, I can totally relate to your alcoholic relatives' behavior, but I live with a man who doesn't touch alcohol. I wish he would drink and pass out late at night then maybe he would leave me alone, but that doesn't happen. Some nights his rants go on for hours. I don't know how long I can take this. How do I cope?" I also shared that his dad was an alcoholic and died from it. I told them that he had said he would never end up like his dad and there would never be alcohol in our home. That was fine with me because there never was much alcohol in my family growing up. Here I was in a room with total strangers who deal with alcohol on a daily basis sharing how they are coping with the behavior of their alcoholics, yet here I am living with the same kind of person who wouldn't dare touch alcohol. I didn't get it! I was confused but also relieved because I was with a group of people who knew exactly what I was going through, and I desperately wanted to understand!

After the meeting, a woman named Barbara came over to me and gave me great big hug. Of course, I was still crying and she said, "I totally understand what you shared and why you are upset. I just want you to know that who you are living with is a person we identify as a 'dry drunk.'" I knew what a bad drunk his dad was from the stories John would share, but I had no idea how badly it had affected him. I became a regular at this chapter of Al-Anon. I worked through the 12 steps with my sponsor, Barbara, over a period of four years. Once I started seeing the light at the end of the tunnel and changing my responses to John's behavior, I was encouraged to get more counseling from my Al-Anon friends. While in Al-Anon I would talk to my mom about her dad's alcohol problem. Mom told me stories of her childhood. Her mother would make her go get him from the bar and beg him to come home. She shared some very disturbing stories that no child should have to go through. Not only did Mom's sharing make me have more empathy for her and grateful that my dad was as wonderful for her as he was, but it also caused me to wonder how my grandmother Roberts could stay in such an abusive situation. I never talked to her about any of this until 10 years later, after John and I ended up divorcing. I went to Fort Worth to visit with her and she shared with me how taboo it was for a Christian woman to divorce back in her day. She told me she was so happy for me to get out of this situation when she was not able to.

My grandfather died in the mid-1980s. After he died, my grandmother blossomed. It was like she was let out of prison. She actually told jokes and laughed a lot. I never heard her laugh like that when I would go over to their home when I was at TCU. She was always grim and on edge. Now I know why! I'm glad I got to come to a place of understanding of her and her story.

During this time, I was taking the girls to Mother's Day Out at Prairie Creek Baptist Church. This gave me several hours on Tuesday and Thursday to pursue my sewing of window treatments to make a little money on the side. One day, I was heading to Dallas to my sister Cheryl's place. She had just graduated from Texas Tech. She wanted me to make some window treatments for her little rent house. It was close to SMU. On the day I headed down there to hang the window coverings, I was praising God in the car on the drive to her place. It was a beautiful time of worship in the car. I was in a very good place. I got the job done and starting packing up my supplies into my car. When I went out to the car I saw that I had a flat tire. I looked at my watch and it was only about 30 minutes until I had to pick up the girls at the church. Before I could finish that thought, an average-sized man came up to me. He looked like a painter in his white overalls. He asked me if I needed any help with the tire. I accepted his offer with pleasure and gratitude. He got it done so quickly that I was on my way and picked up the girls only a little on the late side. I kept thinking about this man and what a godsend he was. I also thought how good my God is and I knew that He was the One who sent the guy. I was once again praising the Lord. I called Cheryl and told her what happened and asked her if there were any painters working near her house about that time. She didn't know, but next day she asked her neighbors on both sides of the street and no one was having any painting done. I was reminded of the verse in Hebrews 13:2 … "Do not neglect to show hospitality to strangers, for by this some have entertained angels without knowing it." I truly believe this helper was an angel. I'll never forget this. God shows up to help his children.

Around 1982, a very strange event happened to our family. We were donors to several Christian ministries. One of those was the 700 Club. This was a very popular Christian network run by Pat Robertson. One day the phone rang and the person on the other line said, "Is this Mrs. Kay Apple?" "Yes, who is this?" "This is the 700 Club calling to thank you and your husband for your dedication in supporting the 700 Club." I said, "You're welcome!" "I am just calling today to ask if you and your family would like to participate in a publicity campaign for the 700 Club and to encourage other young families like yourselves to support us also." I was shocked! Here we were struggling to keep the marriage alive and they wanted to interview us as a family because of our support. I didn't know what to tell him, so all I could say was, "Wow, let me talk to my husband and he will call you back." When John came home I told him what had transpired and he was thrilled. He made the call the next day and got all the information we needed to do this. We told the girls that they were going to be on television, the 700 Club. They were so excited! I bet Lisa thought this would be her moment of fame! March forward 30 days – cameras and sound were setting up in our living room, with vans and trucks crowded in our circular driveway. It was quite an exciting day. We got to watch ourselves on the 700 Club about six weeks later. Of course, friends and family were informed. Through it all, I could hardly believe it because of the darkness that was lurking in our marriage. Glory to God, no matter what!

Shortly after the 700 Club event, I found out I was pregnant again. Lisa was three and Christy was six. I was home-schooling both of them at this point and would continue doing so for the next four years. It was a wonderful experience for me and the girls. They loved it, but as Christy got older she wanted to be at the nearby elementary school where all her neighborhood friends went. Eventually, when we stopped home-schooling, I felt really satisfied that they both got a quality and thorough education. They both thrived when they finally went to Hughston Elementary School several years later.

My pregnancy was uneventful and went by without any hitches. Of course we didn't know what we were going to have, but John wasn't insistent on a boy. He was very realistic and just wanted a healthy, happy baby. On June 30th of 1983, I had lunch with my friend Dena at Taco Bueno. All our kids were at summer camp. As I was leaving the restroom, I felt my water break. I called my obstetrician and he wanted me to come see him. Dr. Dillard told me that I was dilated and it should happen soon. He told me to go shopping, just to walk around until I could feel some contractions. So Dena and I headed south to my favorite children's clothing store, Chocolate Soup. As I was looking around at the goodies, I would feel a contraction. I would lean over the clothing rack and deep breathe. Dena was getting very edgy and nervous. She wanted to get me back to Plano. So we went and picked up the girls at their summer camp. We headed to her house, which was only five minutes from the hospital. The contractions were coming about every 20 minutes. The kids all jumped into the pool and I was lying on her den floor huffing and puffing. She called John and told him that she was taking me to the hospital and to meet us there. I got to the hospital at six that evening. John got there shortly after. Only a few pushes later an 8-pound 15-ounce baby boy arrived, but I saw that he was a little blue with the cord wrapped around his neck. I started praying and John was very nervous. Next thing we know, we hear a very strong bawling baby boy. Johnny Dalton Apple was born June 30, 1983. John and I were so excited to have this little boy with a head full of black hair. I went home the next morning feeling great since there were no drugs in my system – no time for any meds. When we brought him home to the girls, my mom and dad were there to greet us. They were so excited to have a new baby brother and new grandson. The girls were very excited too because Mom and Dad were taking them to Breckenridge for two weeks to give me and baby boy a nice recovery time. All was well with the world, at least for that moment in time.

I have to backtrack a little on this one. Back in the late 1970s in Houston, John was having colitis issues. They continued and got worse. Shortly after our family left Abilene in 1981 for Plano, John's colitis had gotten much worse. He ended up being diagnosed with ulcerative colitis. He was in and out of hospitals for about three years until he eventually had to have his colon removed. My mom had called us and told us about this doctor in Jackson, Mississippi, William Barnett, who had invented a procedure that would create an internal pouch after the colon and rectum were removed. This left the patient with no colostomy bag on the exterior. So off we went to Mississippi in early 1986. Before that trip, I had been volunteering at the Plano Pregnancy Crisis Center. One day I was feeling very queasy and hadn't started my period for a while. I was suspicious but couldn't handle the idea of another pregnancy during all this turmoil. So I took a pregnancy test at the center that day and *voilà!* – I was pregnant. I shared the news with John and he was thrilled. I always thought he just wanted to keep me home and pregnant. I was very upset because our marriage was in such a precarious place. Now with all these things happening I could not see how it would work. I was trusting God for my marriage, John's health and my kids' well-being, especially the one inside of me.

My parents agreed to come to Plano and watch the kids. We left for Jackson, Mississippi. It was in April 1986. I was almost five months pregnant. John had the surgery and was in the hospital for about three weeks. While I was sitting in the hospital with him all this time, I was very interested in the nurses. I was asking a lot of questions. Nursing looked fascinating to me. I remember thinking to myself, "If I ever had to get a job, this is what I would want to do instead of teaching home economics." I had already tried that and I really didn't enjoy it. Also while in Jackson, I looked up some of my junior high friends and got together with a few of them. This made the stay there not so intense. After about three weeks, John was discharged with very detailed care instructions. He and I flew home for his recovery.

Home was now a rent house on Cobbler Street in Dallas. We had moved prior to his surgery because we were needing the income since John hadn't worked for a while. He was still very weak and ill. Recovery was not going very well. He started to have fever and lots of nausea. After speaking to Dr. Barnett, he said that we needed to get him back to Mississippi. Wow! This was getting very hard. So once again my parents cared for the kids, this time in Breckenridge. Once John was in the hospital, they decided he had an infection and some blockages. We ended up staying about a week. When we got home, my mom and dad brought the kids back and we had a chat. They were wanting us to move to Breckenridge and live in their house in town. They were currently living in a trailer out at their new ranch, where they were in the process of building their country dream home. We decided this would be a good move for us, because at this point we did need some help and they wanted to help us. In June of 1986, we left Plano and moved again. When in Breckenridge, we put all our furniture, etc., in a storage unit there. John's recovery was going well this time and I was back to homeschooling the girls. Johnny was about three years old. My pregnancy was going well despite all the chaos. John was back doing some oil and gas work in Breckenridge. It was during this short stay that my parents were seeing how John was treating Christy, which ultimately led to a fight between them and John.

On September 30, 1986, the kids and I took our usual daily afternoon walk around the neighborhood after our home-schooling lessons. Since this was my fourth pregnancy I knew that once I went into labor it would not take long. After the walk I got a call from my mom, "Kay, your dad and I are driving to Dallas because Cheryl is in labor." So off they went to be with Cheryl, my baby sister, when she had her second baby. A couple of hours later, I was in the kitchen fixing dinner and I felt it. Labor was starting. I told John and he took me to the small hospital in Breckenridge. This was around five, before dinner.

I started rather quickly and was dilated pretty good, but then the labor slowed down a bit. John had called Mom at the hospital where Cheryl was and told her I was in labor. She started crying and said, "I've never gotten to be with Kay when she's had a baby and I thought this would be it since y'all were right there in Breckenridge." Cheryl still hadn't delivered either. So there was a phone line set up between my brother-in-law Bob and John. It was a race to the finish to see who would deliver first with my parents right in the middle. At 7:26 PM, Jennifer Lauren Beaudine came into this world a few weeks late. Then at 7:40 PM, James Robert Apple was born a few weeks early! Oh Happy Day! Our little twin cousins. This story made the Breckenridge paper. After Jenny was born, Mom and Dad headed back to Breckenridge. They came to the hospital late, around 11:30 PM to check out the newest grandson. It was only one day in hospital and I was more than ready to come home. Mom was a great help with the new baby and she loved that we were in her town. Life was good after James' birth. No major fights or conflicts. John was loving this new little baby boy. John's health was also improving daily. I had never seen him feel so good since we had been married.

But then, in early November, things got a little more tense and gloomy. John was not liking living in a small town. He started getting into some verbal skirmishes with people in the oil business and some of my parents' friends. You could feel the temperature rising when my parents were around us because they had heard about some of the things he had said and done. All unbeknownst to me. It all came to a head one day when they were over and John started barking at Christy. Well, my dear mom couldn't take his attitude toward Christy as his "Cinderella" anymore. She confronted him.

Dad was also there and he tried to calm things down as usual, but even Dad couldn't control this. He confronted John on some of the rumors he had heard about John's dealings in town. That put John over the edge and he finally yelled and said, "We are getting the hell out of here!" The tears started flowing and everyone was upset, especially the girls. They loved living in Breckenridge. John left and I was there with my kids, parents, and a newborn in my arms. Dad was trying to tell me to just stay here in Breckenridge and let John leave. I really did not want to leave. I told them I would think about it. After they left, John came home and he gave me an ultimatum. "Either you come with me and the kids or you stay here with your mommy and daddy while me and the kids head back to Plano!" I called Mom and Dad and told them that we were leaving the next day. John hired a mover to get all our stuff out of storage and take it to Plano. While all this was happening, I looked down at my wedding ring. I saw that my diamond had fallen out of my engagement ring. That felt like a very bad omen for the future of our relationship.

Somehow John found us a rent house in Plano and we moved in the next day. It was close to Thanksgiving. We had always gone to Breckenridge for that holiday, but we weren't going this year. The girls were very sad. I had not spoken to my mom in about two weeks. So much pain and hurt. Christmas rolled around. Mom called me and asked me if the kids and I would like to be with them and the rest of the family for Christmas. They had rented a big vacation home in Lakeway near Austin. She just couldn't do Christmas in Breckenridge. She was still upset about what had happened. I was too and I told her we would probably stay in Plano. I kept thinking it doesn't have to be this way. I sometimes thought maybe I should have stood up to him and stayed in Breckenridge, not letting him take the kids. Who was I kidding? That would have been impossible in the state he was in and my state was certainly not much better. I was back in Plano and really in need of more counseling and Al-Anon. So, back I went.

1952 - Mom and me, her firstborn, in Fort Worth, Texas

1956 – Kay picking cotton in Throckmorton, Texas

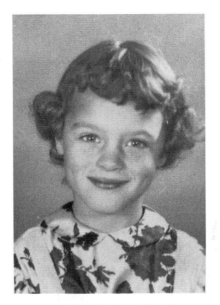

1959 – Kay in 2nd grade at Wolfin Elementary in Amarillo, Texas

1960 – Kay in Eskimo parka staying warm in Calgary, Canada

1963 – Jackson Clarion Ledger front page with Dad holding Cheryl after she was found in the citywide search for her

1963 – Kay, Russell and Cheryl in Jackson, Mississippi

1966 – Freshman at Houston Memorial High School

*1967 – Sophomore year at Houston Westchester
High School with friends*

1969 – Patti R and I in Puerto Vallarta, Mexico with family

1969 – Homecoming Queen Westchester High School with Frank A.

1970 – Westchester High School Senior picture

1972 – TCU Europe Trip in London

*1976 – Grandma and Granddad Whitaker holding first
great-grandbaby, Christy, Kerrville, Texas*

1976 – Mom, me and new baby girl, Christy Kay, Houston, Texas

1979 – Baby Lisa with Grandma and Grandpa Roberts and Mom

1982 – Family Christmas photo in Breckenridge, Texas

1983 – Johnny Dalton with Mom and sister, Lisa

CHAPTER 10

FAMILY GROWING

My steps are established by the Lord and He delights in my
way. When I fall I shall not be hurled headlong because the
Lord is the One who holds my hand.

PSALM 37:23-24

When James was about six months old, I decided to quit home-
schooling the girls again. They were ready and very proficient
in their schoolwork. I was comfortable with that. They had
gotten back with a lot of their previous friends because we
had moved into a rent home only three blocks from our old
home in Plano. We were still in the same school district. John
had decided to go out on his own in the oil business. He did
find a couple of the old guys to go into the business with him.

I had a friend who had just started daycare in her home
and I asked her to watch James a couple of days a week because I was going to go to nursing school. She loved James. I
had also put Johnny in a private Christian preschool. I went
to John and told him that I wanted to go to nursing school. He

said, "No way, you should be home with the kids." I took that as a "no," but since I had the boys in some daycare I decided I wanted to get a job working for John Hancock Insurance Company, delaying the nursing for later, I hoped. I applied without John's knowledge and was hired. I went to all the training programs to get my licenses to sell insurance and mutual funds. I really enjoyed this change in my environment. John was totally not on board with it, but that didn't deter me. My supervisor was a salesman named Bob with an Italian last name. He helped me with cold-calling, training and taught me how to "close the deal!" I had a really great first year. In addition, I was able to connect my dad to some great estate planning attorneys to get him set up with wills, trusts, etc. He was not enjoying this process while it was happening. But when Dad passed away in 2013, all this work really paid off and made dealing with his estate a whole lot easier with all the planning that was done.

One day at work I told Bob that I had a really great sales call that night and to wish me luck. He said, "Better than that, I could meet you there and give you some help." We met at Midway Road and Keller Springs in a shopping center parking lot. I got into his car and off we went to the client's home in Carrollton. After the meeting (and no, I didn't make the sale), he parked his car next to mine to discuss how I could have improved that call. It got quiet. Then the next thing I know Bob is reaching over to grab me for a hug and a kiss. I was flabbergasted. Totally didn't see that coming. "What are you doing?" He said, "I have been wanting to tell you how much I'm starting to like you and I hope the feeling is mutual." In no uncertain terms I let him know how I felt! "This is not right, Bob. I am a wife and a mother of four children just trying to make something out of myself out here in this business world! I can't believe you would try this!" I got out of his car and drove home in mine. I stopped on the way to cry because I just couldn't believe what had happened. I quit the next day and never have told anyone about this until now. The kids were so glad that I was back home with them. Honestly, I was relieved too.

James was growing so fast and becoming quite the character. He loved the fire station up the street. We would walk down there once a week and they would greet him by calling out his name. They would let him put on their hats and boots. Then they would lift him up to sit in the front of the cab of the fire truck. He also loved to go to our bank because they always gave the kiddos some suckers. James was around four at this time, and one day I was looking for him around the house. Our home on Piedra Drive was always filled with kids from the neighborhood. This particular Saturday was very busy with kids and I had not seen little James in a while. I started searching for him. With no success, I asked the kids if they had seen him and no one had. After looking all over the neighborhood, we finally called the police. They called us about an hour later and said they had him. We were so relieved! The police said that apparently James had walked across the four-lane boulevard behind our house to the bank, where he thought he could get a sucker since they always gave him one during the week. Being a Saturday, there was no one in the drive-through. A young couple living in the apartments next door saw the little boy in his Spiderman underwear and called the police. They picked him up and were on their way to bring him home. We all went out to the sidewalk to watch the police car come down the street. I could see James standing up in the back seat of the police car with his arms outstretched on the seat back. He looked like a little prince looking for his kingdom! He was in heaven riding in that police car! We were thrilled to have him back safe and sound.

CHAPTER 11

STEPS TO SANITY

In God's love there is no fear. His perfect love casts out all fear.

1 JOHN 4:18

In quietness and confidence shall be your strength.

ISAIAH 30:15

I was raised in a very innocent and protective environment. I never really knew that there were truly devious and sick people out there in the world. My dad was from a family who only thought good of people and gave them the benefit of the doubt. Later, Mom told me that being raised in Throckmorton made my parents believe in the good of people, because in that tiny little town that's what they did. My mom did have an alcoholic dad. He was an alcoholic ever since she could remember, but she never really talked to me about it until I was in college at TCU. It was then that I started to see what she meant. While I was a sophomore at TCU, I would go to my maternal grandmother's house once a week and take a piano lesson from her, eat supper with them and spend the night. I would go back to TCU for classes the next morning. This was my firsthand experience with addiction in my family. When I was in high school, my boyfriend's family had a lot of alcoholic issues. Many times my boyfriend would tell me how he hadn't gotten any sleep the night before. He had to take care of his toddler brother because his mom and dad were both passed out from alcohol. This kind of thing happened to him a lot.

My granddad was so glad to see me when I would get to their little house in Handley, take my piano lesson and eat Grandma's great cooking. I loved both of them as I was growing up but really never spent much time around them since we lived in so many different places. It was nice to be at one place and see them on a regular basis.

When we had Roberts family gatherings at Grandma and Granddad's house, all of us cousins would always talk about how funny we thought Granddad was. We laughed at him a lot. At this point I never really knew what they knew about him until I started going over there on a more regular basis. When I was there, Granddad would give me the tour of his huge garden and Grandma would show me her quilting projects. She made beautiful quilts. When I would go to bed around 10, I would shut my door. By that time, I had noticed all the empty Falstaff cans in the kitchen trash, so I knew he was drunk. He would knock on my door and stand in the doorway just ranting about how bad my grandmother was and whatever else he was mad about. He would complain about his four daughters, my aunts, and talk about how cruel they were to him. He was always mad at the *Dallas Times*

Herald for cheating him on his retirement or complaining because my mom and dad never came around to see him. I would just agree and say, "Yes, Granddad, I know." While he would be ranting, I would be praying for the Lord to keep me safe and for him to be set free from this problem. I figured he was in this drunken state every night. Now I got just a tiny glimpse at what my mom had to go through as a child with a dad doing this to himself and his family having to endure it.

The next morning Grandma would have a wonderful home-cooked breakfast ready. As I was leaving for TCU, my granddad would load me down with veggies and fruit from his garden and canned goods my grandmother would make. My TCU friends loved all the food I would bring back. Of course nothing was mentioned about what had happened the night before. I had no way to process this except to just keep thinking that Granddad was "funny!"

I hadn't yet grasped the reality of the damage this alcoholic behavior can inflict not only on my mom as a child and an adult child of an alcoholic but also on a grandchild of one.

In Al-Anon, I learned a lot about adult children of alcoholics and how a parent's addiction can affect their behavior. In the meantime, I was changing all my ideas and my behaviors. I was recognizing codependent behavior in myself and trying to change my ways.

My husband, John, was still running his oil and gas business. My dad had once mentioned to me in passing that he thought what John was doing was illegal. My dad actually asked me once if I was signing our tax returns, because they may be fraudulent and if I signed them I was indicting myself. Well, I was too afraid to confront John about this, so I continued to sign them until the very end.

There would be periods of plenty and periods of lack. I could always tell when the money was coming in because John would come home with a car filled with presents for all the kids and they would call it "Christmas in July." One time he came home and told me he had bought all new furniture and paintings and accessories for our living room. It was all coming that afternoon. Of course, it showed up that afternoon and I had no say in it.

I was supposed to feel so fortunate during those prosperous times. John would give me $1,000 in cash and tell me to buy whatever I wanted. But it just felt weird, like a tip. In the meantime, he was adorning himself with Armani clothes and Tag Heuer watches.

It was a strange time and I was learning through counselors what this behavior was showing. *Narcissism* was definitely a word that they would throw out there. I would go home and read about that behavior. It would confirm to me that was what I was living with. It was not healthy for any relationship, but especially a marriage.

As my recovery grew and I got stronger, it continued to totally change the dynamics of our relationship. As I grew from the person who did whatever it took to make him happy, and not rock the boat or say the forbidden word "No," the stress and strain at home became so thick you could definitely feel it. He would actually tell the girls to "Tell your mother that I am not eating that for dinner. I will go get something else." Every day it got worse and worse. It got so bad that when we would turn the corner to head to our house on Piedra Drive, the girls would say aloud and I would be thinking, "Is Dad's car in the front of the house?" We would literally have to prepare ourselves emotionally for him being home and having to deal with whatever lay ahead.

In one instance John asked, "Where are the toothpicks?" in a very accusatory tone. I didn't know and said, "I guess we ran out." Well, he started raging about how it was my job to make sure this kitchen was stocked with whatever we needed! I told him that there was a list on the counter that I had told everyone in the household, including him, to write whatever they needed on this list and I would get it. He ranted, "I'm not putting anything on your list, it is your job to know what we need!" He also began to tell me that he was bringing in his assistant weekly to go through the cabinets and figure out what we needed to buy. Since I was in counseling and getting stronger, I told him, "There's no way Marla is going to rummage through my kitchen!" Lisa, who was about 11, was seeing all this transpire as she was waiting for me to take her to dance. I saw her and realized we had to leave, so I started for the front door with John right behind me yelling at me for my incompetence. I ignored him and kept walking, got into the car and drove off with him standing in the street watching us drive off. While we were driving, Lisa looked at me and asked, "Mom, is Dad mentally retarded?" I just looked at her and said, "No darling, he just has some bad problems." Another time, John implemented the "requisition form" for me to fill out whenever I needed money to buy anything. He created this form that had a place to put what I needed to buy, how much it would cost.

After the shopping was done, I was to provide the receipt for him so he could see if I got cash back! Somehow in spite of my best efforts, I was still in crazy town!

CHAPTER 12

TRUTH REVEALED

You shall know the truth and the truth shall set you free.

JOHN 8:32

No weapon formed against you shall prosper.

ISAIAH 54:17

At this point, another Christian counselor, Les Carter, told me that he believed that John was having an affair. I was horrified because I thought there was no way he would do that. He also told me that he truly believed that John was also a "sociopath" because none of the rules applied to him. This is why he could actually cheat all his oil and gas investors and use their money for purposes that he wanted to, not what he told his clients he would do. Basically "Ponzi Scheming" them. I would think, "How can you treat people like this and not pay for it?" I kept hoping that he was not cheating these people.

I could not wrap my brain around how a person does these things and what ends up happening to people like John.

I remember during all this time, late 1980s-1990, I was hanging onto my spirituality for dear life. It was hard to remember during all of this that He had me all the time. I was reading all my Al-Anon literature, devotionals and the Bible every morning. My devotionals were mostly about codependent behavior. All the information really helped me separate myself from John's behavior and respond to him in a reasonable and sane way instead of the way I had always responded, just to appease. I was getting comfortable with being uncomfortable.

Learning these skills and seeing what all was changing was the best and scariest thing that had ever happened to me. I felt empowered because I wasn't the doormat I had been and I was getting some information outside of me from great counselors.

Then I started going to a great counselor named Rob. He was very confrontative, yet very supportive.

Rob stuck with me for many years and it was such a comfort to have someone as grounded as he was to know all my "shit!" I could go to him and he would confront me on "my part" and basically forget about John Apple. At this point, it wasn't about me and my feelings. It was about me and my responses. How was I responding to what was going on around me? How was it affecting me? Get specific!

This required a lot of work from me that I frankly did not like at all. Confrontation was not something I was comfortable with. The status quo and keeping everyone happy was what I liked. But at this point in my recovery, that was going to be impossible and I knew it. There was going to be a war, and I just prayed that the Lord would enable me to go through this battle because it was worth it for my own sanity and my kids! I kept thinking that I don't want my kids to grow up thinking that my behavior was healthy and end up replicating it in their own relationships. The battle came and God had prepared me through great counseling and a wonderful family!

I also got my hands on a book by Pia Mellody called *Facing Love Addiction*. I read the book and saw my name written in every paragraph.

Life at home wasn't much different than before working. John and I had the modus operandi. After a big emotional, abusive night there would be profuse apologies and making up, with sex mostly. "So sorry, I don't know what I was thinking … forgive me … I love you … don't want to lose you … hug, hug … kiss, kiss … bed … aahhh…" all is well, until the next time. Pretty sicko. This went on until close to the end. After much reading on this topic and counseling, I came to believe the psychosis of this, the symbiotic relationship and response, was my problem. It was love addiction. I had no idea what this meant.

I took the boys to Corpus Christi to a see a friend who had just moved there from Plano and her little girl. James and the little girl were friends from church in Plano. On the way down there, I set the boys up in the back of the Suburban with a small play area to keep them preoccupied. No car movies then and I was the only adult in the car. I was listening to some tapes on "Love Addiction" and finally realized that this was about me, and I finally got it! When we got home from

Corpus, I heard that Pia Mellody was coming to Dallas to speak. I signed up and went to her two-day seminar in Dallas at Lovers Lane Methodist Church. I found myself crying and knowing that this whole seminar defined who I was. It was after this seminar that I called my dad and told him that I was through and wanted somehow to leave John. He was actually very supportive. He said, "I was wondering how long it would take for you to figure this out."

I proceeded to get a great attorney in McKinney and the end began. My attorney was very savvy and understood people like John and how devious they were in order to get what they wanted. He wanted us to get as much information on John as we could, because he knew that he would lie. So he asked me to get him, his computer guy and his paralegal into John's office, which was not far from our home. I was terrified. John never had "let" me come up to his office. I didn't think this would ever happen, but I put on my detective hat and my big-girl panties and trusted the Lord to help me be brave and daring. I called his partner, Mike, and told him that John and I were splitting up and I needed to come to the office when John wasn't there to look around. You could hear his hesitation as he thought about it. I told him that the office was community property and despite what John would tell me, I had a right to come up there.

So the day came for this visit to his office. My attorney, his paralegal and computer guy all met me in the parking lot. We went up to the office and Mike let us in and then left. The team went into speed mode and I just stood back and watched. I could tell these people had done this before. After a couple of hours, as the computer guy was downloading computer files and the paralegal was going through paper files and bank records, the door flies open. There is John Apple standing there in his short-shorts and cut-off tank top with baseball cap on backwards. We were all surprised to see him and interestingly there was no sign of Mike. He had fled after he called John and squealed on us. My attorney went into nice mode. John was on his best behavior, no hysterics, totally in control. I was petrified. Meanwhile, the other two were busy looking for treasured evidence.

Rick, my attorney, walked over to John, shook his hand and introduced himself as my attorney. John, in his diplomatic style, invited us to sit across from him around his big mahogany desk. I was just waiting for the sky to fall, but Rick was very in control. He basically told John that all the information in this office was community property and we needed it for the divorce proceedings. John was equally diplomatic and responded with extreme control, saying, "Nice to meet you, Rick, but I have already filed for divorce and she will be served tomorrow."

Rick responded with, "Just tell your attorney to send the papers to my office. Here is my card." I felt like a picture on the wall while these two men are talking about me and my kids' future. In the meantime, the other two were still busy at work and I saw John nervously watching them as Rick talked to him. In the midst of all this tension, his phone rings on the table behind his desk and he turned to answer it. I was not ready for what I heard. Rick glances over to me as we heard him talking on the phone. "Hey, baby, yeah, I'll be there in an hour or so. Got an emergency here. Talk to you later, baby!"

After that, I was losing it emotionally. I wanted to get out of there. Rick shook John's hand and told him that he would be speaking to John's attorney to try and come to a settlement without a lot of drama. I could not see that happening in the coming months. Of course there was plenty of drama!

So we left the office and I think that John was intimidated by my attorney's suave response to him. Rick gave me the rundown for the future steps we could expect and a timeline. I thanked him and told him I appreciated his calm response as I was l losing it on the inside. He asked if I knew about John's affair and of course I had to say, "No, I never believed it would come to this, but things have been changing really fast lately."

This was around the end of October 1992. John told me he wanted to let the kids know we were divorcing. He wanted to tell them on Halloween night before he had to leave to go to a party. I said, "Fine." I didn't think a quickie announcement with him walking out the door to go partying was the best thing for the kids, but it would totally show him up for who he was. The boys were six and eight and the girls were 12 and 15. I asked the kids to come into the living room in their Halloween costumes. John said, "We are here to let you all know that your mom and I are not going to be able to live together anymore. We are getting a divorce." In response, the boys, being young boys, didn't really understand. They did know that their dad already had an apartment, which I found out about just that night. They asked him if they could come and see him at his apartment. The girls started crying. It was a very sad scenario. With this going on, John announces, "Well, I have to go to my party. I'll see you kids later." The boys asked me, "Mom, can we go trick-or-treating now? Everybody is out there!" So I just agreed and that left me with Lisa and Christy. They were both crying and I tried to reassure them that we were all going to be fine. It was a relief for me. Then Lisa looked up and quit crying. She says to me, "Mom, maybe now you can have a life." These girls were older and saw things the little guys didn't understand. I agreed with her. Then Christy said, "You mean Dad really isn't going to be around here anymore?" I told her, "Yes, that's it."

She responded with, "It is going to be like getting out of prison. I don't have to worry if he will be here anymore when I get home from school?" I told her, "He will not be here anymore when you get home. It is going to be a big change for all of us. We won't have to make things okay to make him happy. He's gone, gone, gone!"

CHAPTER 13

STARTING OVER

For He knows the plans He has for you, plans for welfare and
not calamity, to give you a future and a hope.

JEREMIAH 29:11

I shared what was going on with my small group from our church. It was an eye-opener for me. A few of the women in my group knew some of what was going on in my marriage, but the men were not very aware. Once I announced to the group that John and I were divorcing, it was met with some consternation. They prayed for us, but other than that not much was shared. I don't think they could handle this big of a problem in their group. Next day I got a phone call from the leader of our group. He was a nice guy with two young girls. His wife was my friend. He started lecturing me on what "the Word" said about divorce. Like I didn't already know. He said, "Kay, you should stay in this marriage and pray." It was like a slap in the face and very upsetting to me physically and emotionally. I told him, "I know what the Word says, and for one thing you have no idea what you are talking about, and you know nothing about what is going on!" John had not been in the group for about a year, so this guy really had no idea who John was. And as I recall, he never reached out to him either. Not that it would have made any difference at that point. I was so turned off by this kind of religious know-it-all. This might be coming from good hearts, but little do they know the pain that it causes the person they are preaching to. Especially when they don't know the details and don't even ask.

I called my dad and shared what had happened with the group leader. He wanted his phone number and said he wanted to share some information with him. I had no idea what he was going to say. Later he called me and said, "Well, I think I have straightened this guy out. Who does he think he is, telling you what you should do or not do? If I were you, I wouldn't return to that group, but I would keep going to Al-Anon where you will get a lot less judgment than you will from the church."

In dealing with such people and ideas, I would usually cry and feel guilty and doubt myself. I would think this was going to be a bad move for my kids, but deep down I knew that staying with this narcissistic sociopath was not the life I wanted for me or my children. I knew that he would always be their dad and that they would have to deal with all the pain and loss from their own relationship with him. Actually, many years after the divorce when the kids were getting older, I told them that I would help them out by paying for counselors when they felt like they needed them. I knew they would be needing it in their futures.

Right after the divorce I started taking the kids to the Rainbow program. It was like an Al-Anon for children. They loved it and were learning ideas of how to cope with difficult people. For example, when another person is treating them wrong, it is okay to detach from that person and know that "whatever bad things this person is telling you is more about them than about you." I would talk to my kids about God and that He is all about love and forgiveness. He never wants any harm to come to you. This is a world where there is pain and all must walk that path at some time in our lives. When it does come to you or hard decisions need to be made, just take it one step at a time knowing that your Heavenly Father will guide you to the best decision. This a lesson my kids would hear from me over and over again for many years, even up to this very day. So I took my dad's advice and stopped going to the group and continued with Al-Anon, where I was growing with the Twelve Steps program. It was during this time that my spiritual life took a turn. I knew that I had a lot of growing to do and I needed help to navigate the road ahead of me. Divorced again, supporting and raising four children was a job I believed, with the Lord's help, I was ready to take on. Actually, I was encouraged because at this point the only person stopping me from growing and moving forward was me, myself and I.

So the divorce process started and involved all the usual divorce scenarios. Before we had our last meeting with attorneys to sign the papers, I had started getting my nails done and got my hair highlighted. These were two things that John never would allow me to do or spend the money on. It was a big deal to me because it represented my newfound freedom.

When we were going over the agreement, I would use my new nails to point out things on the decree I agreed with. I know this sounds petty, but it was symbolic to me of my good feelings and my freedom.

There were problems with abiding by the agreement because someone like John didn't abide by any rules except his. I was still in a lot of counseling to help me with my responses and keeping my boundaries. The boys became John's pawn in all this. The girls were not interested in all the goodies that he would promise them like the boys were. John lured them with lots of toys, trips and pretty much whatever they wanted. This made parenting harder for me. I started taking the boys to Dr. Paul Warren at Minirth-Meier Clinic, where they started to understand some of what their dad would do to keep them "on his side." This is a typical divorce problem with kids. He would not abide by visitation agreements. Keeping the boys past the weekend and not bringing them home left me with no option but to call the sheriff to go get the boys and bring them home.

In December 1992, our divorce was final. There was a lot of lying about his income numbers as far as setting up child support for the four kids. But in exchange, like Christy said, we never had to deal with his moods, so it really was like being set free from prison.

I was not working at this time because I was looking at going back to school to get my Registered Nurse's license. In January 1993, I enrolled in nursing school at Collin County Community College. I was so excited to go in this direction for my career. It was such an adventure and I went at it with full speed ahead. Since I already had a degree from TCU, a lot of courses were already on my transcript. It only took me two and a half years to get my license and start working as an RN.

During this time at school I started going out with some of my new social single friends. It was a totally foreign world for me but I was having fun. The kids would go with their dad every other weekend, except Christy, and sometimes Lisa.

This period for me is not a time I am proud of because I wasn't going to church, and because I was fed up with the hypocrisy of what I had experienced in the church. I was looking for fun and to be free. My girls were still involved in their youth group and the boys were rarely, if ever, going to church. I saw myself as turning away from religious hypocrites like John had been. I wanted to find love again, but this time it was not going to be with anyone like John. I wanted someone who knew how to be my friend. I was in a very vulnerable place, but getting stronger every day.

Right after my divorce was final, my nail person wanted me to go with her and some friends to a country-western place in east Richardson called Fairfield's. Country-western was really big in the early nineties. I said I would be there. John and I had been there a few times right toward the end of the marriage. I think it was where he picked up his next wife. But I said yes anyway! I didn't have any kids that weekend and was ready to start having some fun. I got there around nine o'clock. The band was playing. You could tell that most of the crowd there were regulars. A live band was on the stage. There was a softball team over to the side playing darts, with a square dance group getting out on the floor every other song to show off their dancing and twirling skills. My friends and I were ordering our wine and beer and the band started up again. There was a great fiddle player in the band. I was watching him play his fiddle when I got a tap on my shoulder and I hear a stuttering voice say, "W-w-would you like to d-d-dance with me?" Of course I turned around and said yes to this much younger man. When I said yes, my friend grabbed my wrist and tried to stop me. I couldn't understand why and went with him to the dance floor. We started doing the so-called two-step to the beat of the band. I could tell that something was wrong after the first two or three steps. We were the only ones on the dance floor and as the music continued, the dance was becoming more irregular to the rhythm. Instead of shuffling along with ease there were these staccato moves to our dancing. I said to him, "Do you think we could pick it up a bit?" In a stuttering voice he said to me, "No, this is the b-b-best I can do." At this point I realized why my friend pulled on my wrist to try to stop me. Apparently everyone who were regulars at Fairfield's knew this kid. But I was in it, so I just went with it and finished the whole dance with him. It actually wasn't as bad as my friends thought it was. I could see from the looks of everyone watching us that not many people would dance with him. He was just a sweet mentally challenged kid who wanted to have some fun and I was there to provide it. As we would circle around the floor together the softball team was watching and the square dancers were intrigued.

The fiddle player was especially loving this, as he would wink at me when we would pass by in our floor rotation. After the song was over, I thanked the kid for the dance and went back to my friends and my glass of wine. They were saying, "Kay, we tried to warn you." I replied, "Hey, you guys, it's okay, the kid just wanted a dance. I had a good time and entertained all you guys!" The square dance couples came to the table and told me how sweet I was to dance with the kid, then the softball players came over and gave me a hug for dancing with him. I was beginning to feel like a hero! When the band took their break, the fiddle player came over and asked me out because he thought I must be some pretty special person to dance with the kid for a whole song. I told him thanks but no. I was old enough to be his mother!

CHAPTER 14

NEW CAREER

God, being rich in mercy, because of His great love with which
He loved me, even when I was dead in my trespasses, made
me alive together with Christ (by grace I have been saved),
and raised me up with Him and seated me with Him in the
heavenly places, in Christ Jesus, in order that in the ages to
come He might show the surpassing riches of His grace in
kindness toward us in Christ Jesus.

EPHESIANS 2:4-7

One night in the winter of 1993, a friend of mine from high school, Nancy E, asked me to go country-western dancing with her and some friends. It was there that I met my next love. He asked me to dance. He was a great dancer. This led to us meeting once a week at this dance place and developing a relationship. He taught me how to play golf. We always had so much fun. Of course there were red flags, but I just wouldn't stop the train. During our dating days, I became friends with the wife of one of his friends from work. Her name was Kitty and she and I became close. We would go on double dates with Kitty and her husband, Gary. She shared with me one day that she knew that Duyane was quite the ladies' man, but she could tell he was really crazy about me. She hoped it would all work out because she loved being around me and I with her.

We had lots of fun doing many different things. Duyane would take me to lots of concerts. We saw Jimmy Buffett, the Eagles, George Strait, ZZ Top and many others. He liked to have this kind of fun. Lots of music, drinking and partying. We went on a lot of trips to Mexico once we got married. Lots of partying down there. And there was lots of golfing. So I could check the fun box off with him.

We eventually got married in June 1995 and bought a house together in Arlington. I sold my Plano home and moved three of my kids to Arlington for a "new start." My oldest was already going to school at Texas Tech and barely came home during the year because she wasn't a fan of my new husband. She ended up spending a lot of time with her grandparents in Breckenridge on her off weekends from Texas Tech.

James made quick friends with his lifetime buddies, the Bothe boys, just one house down on our cul-de-sac. He was in elementary school and Johnny was in middle school at the time. It was harder for him to adjust. Lisa was 16 and a junior at Mansfield High School. She immediately got involved in the fine arts choir program.

I was working full-time as an RN at Arlington Memorial and then at Medical Center of Arlington. I loved going to work because every day, nursing offered new challenges with new people to take care of. I was a good nurse and made a lot of new friends from work. Helping people get well and seeing quick recovery of people who had very serious illnesses in the ICU and Cath Lab was very rewarding.

When I went back to school after my divorce from John in 1993, I was so filled with excitement. Every day, I was in awe of what I was learning. The biology, anatomy, statistics, clinicals and labs were so invigorating. I felt empowered to be doing something I knew I was ready and willing to do. It was not easy with four kids still at home. The youngest was in kindergarten and Christy was a senior in high school.

Going to Collin County Community College was a true blessing because their nursing school gave us so much hands-on experience in our clinicals in the hospitals. On my first nursing job at Arlington Memorial Pediatric floor, I was interning with another fresh grad from TCU nursing school. The head nurse, MaryAnne, told me and Michele to go start a couple of IVs on some patients going in for procedures. Needless to say, I was so excited, but when we got into the supply room to get what we needed, Michele had this "deer in the headlights" look on her face. I asked, "What's wrong?" She replied, "I have no idea what to get or how to start an IV!" I was flabbergasted that a graduate nurse from my alma mater was so ill-prepared for the floor job of a nurse. I told her not to worry. I proceeded to gather what we needed and started the IVs. As she watched and learned, I assured her that I would work with her. She eventually became very proficient at it. Another fun story was when I was assigned to have my first clinical rotation at Plano General Hospital. I walked in bright and early to the ER where there were nurses and aides sitting around the station. They probably were a little shocked that this student was at least 15 years older than them and was as eager as a cheerleader at a playoff game! I announced to them who I was and was ready to get to work. "What can I do?" All the seasoned head nurse said was, "Make her presentable to her family." The head nurse pointed to curtain six. I said, "Sure!" So I headed over, pulled the curtain and closed it. Right in front of me was an elderly woman who was dead with tubes coming out of every orifice of her body. I felt very sad for the family. Since I had never touched a dead body before, I proceeded to "glove up" and get started. With gentleness and care I proceeded to remove all the tubes and place dry bandages where needed. I gave her a bath and fixed up her hair. I changed her sheets and got her a clean gown. It took me more than an hour. I stood back after I was done and smiled knowing that her family would not be so sad because now she just looked like she was sleeping. I walked out of the curtained room and nodded. The seasoned nurse, who dutifully had to check my work, walked in and then came out to where I was. She gave me a thumbs up. There is nothing better than knowing you've done a good job!

On 9/11, I was working my day shift in ICU at Medical Center of Arlington. It was around 7:15 in the morning right after shift change. I went to ICU room eight to take care of a patient I had the day before. I was chastising him for his high blood pressure. This wasn't his first time to be my patient. He was a repeat offender. He didn't want to quit smoking or drinking and refused to take his meds. His wife was sitting in the room watching the news. As I was waiting for the blood pressure cuff to deflate, I saw it all on the news. The first tower down, the planes running into the towers, the chaos. I ran outside of his room and shouted, "Everyone get to a TV. The Twin Towers are down!" I kept shouting that this is the job of Osama Bin Laden. Some were asking me who the heck he was and I told them. I had learned about him from keeping up with Al Qaeda terrorist attacks on the news and thought, "It's got to be this guy!" The rest of the 12-hour shift that day was filled with angst and anxiety for all the patients and nurses. I'm sure my patient in room eight's blood pressure never went down all that day, even with me giving him his meds.

Another work incident I won't forget is a 90-year-old patient I had who was near death as I started my shift. I felt the need to call her son and let him know. He told me, "I'm not interested in this. We are not close and I'm not coming to the hospital!" Click – he hung up. I was shocked that a son could be so callous. I took care of her and made her as comfortable as possible but she ended up dying around noon. I talked to Scot, the head nurse, and I told him that I had no one else to call from her family because I had already called the son and he was not interested. So he just told me to clean her up. He would call the morgue downstairs. I proceeded to do the cleanup and once she was ready, Scot was at the door to her room with a gurney. He and I placed her lifeless little body on the gurney and covered her with a sheet. I had tears in my eyes for her. Being so family-oriented, I can't imagine the pain in a family's heart who treat each other like this. So sad and unnecessary. I asked Scot where we were taking her and he said, "The morgue downstairs." I had never been inside the morgue, much less delivered a body to it. All the patients I had up until then had family. When they died, we would just call the selected funeral home. They would come and pick up the body to prepare for burial. As we approached the morgue in the basement, I could feel how sterile, lifeless and dreary it was. We walked in and Scot opened up a small door and pulled out a stainless steel box. He tells me, "Okay, Kay, we have to put her in this." I am bawling at this point and can't keep from crying. Scot could tell this was my first time in the morgue.

Then there is the story of the family who were lovingly surrounding their dying mom in the ICU. They were telling me stories about her. They told me they were sure that she would never go until she saw her son who was overseas. I told them that we had to transfer their mom to a Med/Surg floor upstairs for hospice care because she no longer needed ICU services. I had spent a lot of time talking to this lady's family about her and how much they loved her. She was in a coma and they knew she didn't have long to live. They told me that her son was on his way to see her and say goodbye. They truly believed that she would stay alive to say goodbye to her son. I told them I believed that she would too. So I got her all set and took her to the Med/Surg floor and made her comfortable. I told the family that I was going to be off for two days but I would come up and check on her when I was back on duty. When I came back, I went upstairs and talked to the head nurse. She told me that the son had come to see her yesterday and a couple hours later, with her whole family there, she gave up the ghost. The nurse said it was a very sweet goodbye. There is a lot of spirituality in stories like this. They happen often in a hospital setting if you are sensitive to it, because the human spirit is so strong and beliefs are so powerful.

On a lighter note: We had a great Head RN on Medical Center of Arlington's ICU, Scot from Wisconsin. He really had no family ties and was always kidding me and telling me, "Kay, I think you must know and/or be related to everyone in Texas!" "Of course," I told him, "If you had lived in as many places in Texas as I have and been a fifth-generation Texan you would too!" So on one of many days, I was typing my patient notes on my computer, minding my own business, but still listening to Scot and our Biotech guy, "Bio Joe" from who knows where, talking at the counter right above me. I started listening to these two amigos talking about Bio Joe's great hunting weekend.

Neither of these guys are Texans. Joe was so impressed with his hunting weekend because the guide was awesome and they shot a lot of deer. I just had to stop typing, focus and listen to his story. Finally, I had to ask, "Hey Joe, where were you hunting?" He replied, "Throckmorton County." I knew this was going to freak Scot out so I kept going. "Who was your hunting guide?" Of course I knew what his answer was going to be. At this point I am loving this. Joe's answer was "Brad Whitaker." I replied, "That's my cousin Brad!" At this point Scot, from Wisconsin, went crazy yelling, "You really are related to everybody in Texas!" And of course I said, "Yes, I am!"

While I was at Medical Center of Arlington, they were starting a publicity campaign for the hospital. The head of Nursing Administration, who hired me away from Arlington Memorial, asked if I would be interested in being a part of this campaign, involving billboards, newspapers, TV and radio. How could I say no! It sounded like a lot of fun, so we started. There were three other nurses chosen from different areas of the hospital. The campaign went public and sure enough my big headshot was in the *Fort Worth Star-Telegram*, a small TV commercial with me and a patient, and a billboard on highway 360-N with me and the other three nurses. Always with a big smile on our faces. I didn't make a big deal about it to my kids. But my husband, Duyane, was so excited. James' buddies were asking him about his mom's picture in the paper. All of Duyane's friends were kidding him that his wife's picture was plastered in the *Star-Telegram*. But the funniest was, one weekend Johnny came down from his dad's place in Plano to stay with us for the weekend. On his way back on 360-N, he stopped and called me yelling and freaking out, "Mom, I'm looking up and seeing this huge picture of you on a billboard!" I told him all about it.

I always told my patients, "If you are a patient of mine at MCA, I guarantee you will be well taken care of!" I hate to brag, but I loved that job, the people I took care of and the people I worked with.

I will just share one more story about the most favorite of all the people I worked with at MCA. When I first came to MCA ICU, I knew no one in the whole hospital except the guy who hired me. So on my first day on the ICU, I saw my patients' doctors were putting their charts up on the ledge by the secretary's desk. When I was at Arlington Memorial I learned how to input my own patients orders in the computer because there was a shortage of unit secretaries.

I thought I would help out and grab my charts and do my own orders. BIG MISTAKE! The doctors there knew where to put the charts with their new orders ... right in front of

Ina's desk, the unit secretary. Well, no one shared this tidbit of information with me! So being the independent person I am, I reach for one of my patient's chart and this hand slaps the counter where I'm reaching. This voice says, "What are you doing?" in a rather angry tone. Of course I had not met her yet, seeing as this was my first day in the ICU. I just said, "Well, I thought I would put my own orders in!" I got my baptism that day into the ICU and learned who ran the joint! Her name was Ina and she is one of the best unit secretaries I've ever worked with. We have become best friends since that incident. She has loved my children, as I have loved hers. We shared a lot of kid stories at lunch break, which we always tried to have together. She loved for me to tell her funny stories of James and Johnny. She was crazy about James and was one of the sweetest supporters and saddest ones when he died. Life is so great because of the people the Lord brings along your path. My motto is "Stay open, because you never know!"

While all this was going on, I knew that I wasn't in relation with the Lord like I had been. It was getting hard dealing with John Apple because not only did he not follow any rules, but after I had been remarried for a year, he completely stopped sending the child support checks. In the meantime, he had remarried two years prior to that. I asked him why he stopped abiding by the court order. He said, "Now that that you are remarried, you don't need it!" I was shocked he thought he could get away with that. So I was out looking for an attorney again. I didn't find a good one; however, John got the meanest divorce attorney in Fort Worth. It was a year of lie after lie on his part. I had to do all the research to prove he was lying. It totally consumed my life and my thoughts. Also, he had decided not to help any of the kids with cars or college. So the girls were helped by their Papa when it came time to go to college.

They hardly ever saw John. The boys would see him on regular visitations. John and his new wife had moved to Arlington. It made it easier to get the boys on his weekends. John and his new wife, Ashley, had a new baby boy.

In the meantime, Johnny was not making his grades in ninth grade, and I told him if he didn't start making better grades there would be no drivers ed or license. So conflict was high in our house with the court case and Johnny's grades.

The way this all ended after a year of court hearings and subpoenas was the judge asked us to do mediation. She actually told me that if we didn't work this out I would be the one to pay John child support. Her reasoning was that she believed John's lies about his $22,000 per year income. My income was just slightly more than that. During that year, I presented witnesses who testified about John's dishonest promises to them and gave evidence of his expenses and possessions. She chose to not believe any of it. I gave up and Johnny ended up moving in with his dad, who had promised him he could get his driver's license and a new car. I would keep James with no child support from John. It was an "even swap!" What a waste 2001 was, with no fair results and lots of attorney fees.

During all this ordeal, my sweet Grandma Whitaker passed away from septicemia in an arm infection. This hit us pretty hard, but I know she was glad to move on and be with Granddad.

1987 – James on the piano, Plano, Texas

1989 – James in one of many costumes

1993 – Family portrait after divorce

1996 – James with cousin Wesley, painting fences
in Breckenridge, Texas

1995 – James playing guitar in neighborhood, Arlington, Texas

*1993 – James, Grandma Whitaker and me in
Breckenridge, Texas*

*James hunting dove with Papa and me, as the retriever,
in Breckenridge, Texas*

1996 – Cousins making memories in Breckenridge, Texas

1996 – Happy James in Breckenridge, Texas

*2001 – Johnny at high school graduation with Mama and
Papa in Plano, Texas*

2003 – Rock 'n' Roll Marathon in San Diego, California

2003 – James' Graduation celebration with Tanson and Trey

2003 – Family trip in Las Vegas, Hoover Dam

CHAPTER 15

BETRAYED AGAIN

You shall know the truth and the truth shall set you free.
JOHN 8:32

Peace I leave with you, My peace I give to you.
Not as the world gives do I give unto you. Let not your
heart be troubled, nor let it be fearful.
JOHN 14:27

It was 1997 and all I had at home with me was Duyane and James. The three of us got along great. Lisa was off to college at Belmont University in Nashville, Tennessee. Christy had graduated from Texas Tech and got a great job in Dallas. Johnny was living with his dad.

In Christy's senior year at Texas Tech, around the holidays, she called me in tears. I asked her, "What's going on?" She said, "I just got a box of Christmas ornaments from my real dad's mother, Eunice." I was shocked. She was obviously upset and sad. I couldn't quite figure out how all this had happened.

I didn't realize she had made some connections in Lubbock with Steve's sister-in-laws, who were big names in Lubbock. They informed Eunice of Christy's address at her Tech apartment and thus was the beginning of her getting to know her paternal grandmother. This relationship has grown slowly and steadily. Christy was very cautious and scared. Through the next several years she ended up meeting her grandmother Eunice on some of her business trips. On one particular visit, Eunice set up a meeting for Christy to meet Steve, her real dad, in Florida. Christy told her she would go but was not looking forward to it. I was praying for her when she let me know that she was about to meet him. After it was over, she called me and said, "I did it, Mom, and it was weird!" I asked her why. She said that when Eunice got them together, he gave her a big hug and said, "Oh, my sweet baby girl!" Christy said it was so weird to have this man she had never seen before and never knew about him until she was five years old hug her and act so loving. She told me, "I never want to see him again." I said, "You can do whatever makes you comfortable." She still kept in touch with her grandmother Eunice, but very limited. I was sad and glad for her because she made some contact with her true roots. I knew that it would be good for her to have some history and not be clueless about her real father.

Life went on with me at work and I started to remodel our kitchen. I did all the painting myself. Duyane seemed to be spending a lot more time at work and was coming home later than usual. There was a time when he would come home as soon as he could and we would go play golf or we would cook dinner together. Things were different. I really couldn't tell what was going on with him. I asked one day why he was working so much longer. Was he on a special project or what? He casually mentioned that the company he worked for had assigned him a 23-year-old intern to mentor. Then later on he told me the intern was a female. I told him I was very uncomfortable with that and wanted him to quit as a mentor. I knew about his philandering and girl chasing in the past before me, but he always made me feel so secure in our relationship. I shared this with my girlfriend, Kitty, and she assured me that he was so in love with me that he would never cheat on me, especially with a 23-year-old. I chose to believe that. Let me add that he had a 24-year-old daughter from his previous marriage. I just stayed busy working and remodeling our kitchen. One day he told me that he was going to Atlanta for a business trip. I asked who was going and he told me that Joanna, his intern, was going, but it was all "okay." This was a very nerve-wracking time for me. It brought back my past feelings of suspicions and betrayals. I gave him the benefit of the doubt. Right before this time I had reconnected with my TCU friend, Janice, and was invited to her oldest daughter Ashley's wedding in downtown Fort Worth. Duyane told me that he would meet me at the wedding after he landed at the airport when he got back. When he was late showing up, I called him and he said that when "they" got in they were hungry so "they" went to get some dinner. He was going to take her home then go back home and skip the wedding. I was shaking because this really unnerved me. When I got home, I told him how upset I was that he didn't show up for the wedding, instead eating out with "Joanna." To add fuel to the fire, I kept remembering that the woman John had the affair with at the time of our divorce was named Joanna. It was getting to be too much. He assured me that "Everything is okay, not to worry." One afternoon he asked me if I would go get his cellphone out of his car. I did and while I was looking for it I ran across a receipt from some restaurant in Atlanta where the trip happened. I saw the receipt for a meal Vought Aircraft paid for and it looked like a very romantic menu for two, but I didn't say anything at the time. My suspicions were very high at this point.

Every year we went to the Fort Worth Stock Show and Rodeo on the last weekend of the rodeo, usually the first week in February. My parents would come to town and a few of my cousins would go with us. All of my kids would go and some cousins would show up. It was a tradition since I was a freshman at TCU when I would go with my granddad. All was well, we were having a great time with all the little kids, nieces and nephews. The night was over. We had all come home and gone to bed. I was downstairs wondering where Duyane was. His office was upstairs. I saw the light on upstairs and I quietly went sneaking up the stairs, because deep down I didn't trust him. I had my suspicions. As I walked into his office, with his back to me, I was able to read over his shoulder without him even knowing I was there. He must have been so enthralled with the 23-year-old's emails. It was then that I saw the email from Joanna saying, "I can't wait for us to get married and I can have your babies!" I gasped so loud it got him out of his stupor, and he said, "It's not what you think, Kay. It really isn't!

What I had been suspecting was true. Now it was all making sense. Staying out in the car on the cellphone once he gets home, birthday parties for people from work that I don't know. I can't even describe the pain and the anger that erupted from me. Duyane was a very big guy and I just started hitting him with my fists. He was shocked to see me behind him and accusing him of cheating. He was sorry that he got caught and started apologizing and saying, "It's no big deal!" I was hysterical and ran back downstairs. I was totally caught off guard and didn't know how to react. Do I be calm or go crazy? I went crazy. That night, I never slept. He kept denying this until I started looking at his cellphone bill. All the evidence pointed to lots of phone calls and an affair with a 23-year-old. The next day I went to see my best friend, Kitty, whose husband was a vice president of the company and a friend of Duyane's. She said she had heard rumors of his mentee but had never met her at the office. I felt so betrayed that she didn't tell me. She apologized and said she was there for me, and she was till the end of this relationship. In the meantime, I kicked him out of the house because he refused to go to counseling and said he was happy with her. I was betrayed again. How does this keep happening? I went back to my counselor, Rob, in Dallas. I saw him every week for the next six months. My husband was only disappointed that he got caught, not about what he had done. Seems like everyone at the company he worked at knew that he was cheating and no one had the nerve to tell me.

I was hell-bent on finding the most ball-breaking attorney in Arlington. I found her, Stephanie Foster. She was something else. I just wished I would have had her when I took John Apple to court for back child support. We proceeded to hardball this divorce and it all ended about eight months later. I was more hurt in this divorce than any other. It was the saddest time of any of my marriages because I really loved and liked him. I believed that he loved me. We went on trips with friends, played lots of couples golf together, cooked together and liked each other. The element of controlling and backstabbing was not there. I wasn't afraid to come home when his truck was in driveway. I was glad that he was home. In my other divorces I knew that they were over after a period of time, but this one hit me between the eyes and shocked me. Even during those eight months before the divorce was final I would cry every night out by the pool. It was only James and me at the house. He was about 16 at the time and going through his own struggles with school. Now he was having me go through another painful breakup. This was hard on him. His friends have shared with me how James would tell them how sorry he was that his mom had to go through this again. We would sit, cry and hold each other out by the pool on some nights. Took me a long time to recover from the pain. I knew that my decision to say yes to him eight years before was not a good thing because I didn't believe that his tendency for running around would happen to me. He acted like he was so crazy about me that I thought this would never happen. Fooled again.

I immersed myself in work during this recovery time and continued to see my counselor, Rob. Even James would go see Rob occasionally.

Johnny had been having trouble with his dad. He moved in with him his sophomore year. They moved back to Plano, where Johnny went to high school. Once he was a senior at Plano Senior High, his dad kicked him out of his house for some selfish reason on John's part. It was a mess. Johnny really didn't want to move back to Arlington but wanted to finish high school in Plano, then move back to Arlington and live with me and James. He had some great friends whose parents let him live with them until he graduated. God is so good and you can never predict how things will work out – they just do in one way or the other! I figured that at this point Johnny was seeing the truth about his dad and knew that it was a losing battle to try and make sense of it all. So when he graduated from Plano Senior High School, he moved back in with me and James in Arlington in 2002. I knew at this point that Johnny had come to the "Aha" moment of who his dad really was. I never had to say anything. This had happened with Christy and Lisa, now finally with Johnny. The last one to figure it out was James.

CHAPTER 16

SINGLE ADVENTURES

By His doing you are in Christ Jesus,
who became to us wisdom from God, unto righteousness
and sanctification and redemption.
1 CORINTHIANS 1:30

Things which eye has not seen and ear has not heard, and
which have not entered the heart of man, all that God has
prepared for those who love Him.
1 CORINTHIANS 2:9

It was fall of 2003 and I was single again. James was 16 and struggling with school. Johnny was back in Arlington with us and going to Tarrant County Community College.

At this juncture, I just didn't want to go to bars to meet anyone! Been there, done that! I kept busy with work and went to Nashville to see Lisa a lot. She was a music student at Belmont University. A trip to Nashville was a lot of fun for me. There was so much to do! Christy was working at a sports marketing company in Dallas and seemed to be doing okay. One day Johnny said, "Mom, you really need to get out and have some fun." All the people I socialized with when married to Duyane faded away after the divorce, so the social scene was scarce except for Kitty and my nursing friends from work. I was still playing golf with a few friends but it wasn't the same. I checked out the newspaper and found that there was a Single Gourmet club for singles who enjoyed fine dining. That was for me, so I signed up! We met once a month at really fabulous restaurants from Fort Worth to Dallas! I met some great people and ate some delicious food. I also joined the DFW chapter of the American Singles Golf Association. This group became my lifeline for new friends and fun trips! My first visit to the DFW chapter of ASGA was at a big sports bar in Dallas. There was a crowd of singles there. As soon as I walked in, this bombshell blonde who looked like Cybill Shepherd walked up to me, put her arm around me and said, "I need your vote. I am running for president of this chapter of ASGA. My name is Pam Porter!" The 6-foot-tall woman took off to find more voters! I left there looking around for a drink and do some mingling. Needless to say, Pam became president. I joined that night and we are still great friends! As a group, we would play golf once a month at various courses throughout the DFW area and have a Happy Hour once a month. There was a bigger national ASGA organization and they sponsored trips to great locations. I ended up going on several of these trips during my single years.

My first adventure with the ASGA national organization was a trip by myself to Palm Springs. They had a huge chapter and it sounded really fun, so I signed up to go. I flew by myself, and when I got there I rented a Mustang convertible, with my luggage and clubs in the back seat! I have to say I was in hog heaven, because I was on my own having a great time. I got a room at a retro-fifties renovated motel. My room's patio door opened to the pool and a grassy area. After I got settled I started walking around the grounds. I heard all these girl voices a few rooms up from mine. I went toward the voices and came upon a group of six girls smoking and drinking on the patio. I was so excited to see these ladies, I just spoke out, "Hey y'all." They all looked me over and said, "Y'all?" Then they start laughing and asked me if I was from Texas. Of course I said yes. They invited me to have a seat and a drink. I gladly did because I didn't know anyone on this trip. I was open to meet anyone who looked nice and fun! I had a great time laughing and visiting with them. They were all from Phoenix and were in Palm Springs for the ASGA golf weekend. That night there was a happy hour and dinner at a local restaurant! We agreed to meet up there. When I got to the restaurant and started looking for them in the sunken area where the group was seated, all I saw was a sea of white and silver hair! I kept looking and I finally saw the Phoenix girls in the back left corner of the room. I beelined over to them. We were all about 20 years younger than the rest of the folks. After the dinner festivities were over, there was talk about going to Mel's, which was an old club where Dean Martin, Frank Sinatra and the proverbial "Rat Pack" hung out! I was excited, so of course I said I was in. I got back into my Mustang and headed over there, which was very close by. Once I got there, I saw my new Phoenix girlfriends and others starting to dance to the great band that was playing. An older gentleman approached me. He had silver hair and asked me to dance. I rarely say no to a dance invite! The gentleman seemed to be a very savvy dancer. We pulled some really lofty moves, and I must say I was impressed with his agility. The night went on. After much fun, I knew I should leave because there was a nine o'clock tee time at a local course the next morning. I arrived at the course early to check in to play golf. I asked the local lady checking me in where the guy was that I danced with the night before. She looked up at me and seriously said, "He's is not here today because his back went out after so much dancing last night!" I felt terrible and I never saw the guy again the whole weekend! But overall it was a great time for me. I made some good friends from Phoenix. I ended up playing golf and seeing my new friends there a couple of months later on another fun ASGA trip.

I also went with my new ASGA girl and guy friends from Dallas to The Homestead in Virginia. There were also trips to Seattle and Vancouver. With my nursing schedule, I could work three 12-hour shifts in a row and that left me with seven days free. I decided that I was going to travel while in this phase of life. These ladies became my lifelong friends. We went through all of this together and laughed our way through most of our fiascos!

At this point in life, why take everything so seriously! Seriously! There were a lot of events during this time in my life that I could document, but I think that it would truly show how lost I was in my life and my relationship with Jesus. He knew what I was going through and I knew deep down that He also knew I saw myself like I saw my kids. You will get through this and come out okay on the other side. There was one incident during this period around 2004 that stands out as the epitome of these single years of mine. My two besties were Lynette and Pammy. Pammy was my singles coach because she had been single the longest and knew all the rules. Lynette was kind of like me, just ready to have a good time! So the girls decided that a group of us from ASGA needed to go to Bass Hall for a Michael McDonald and Steve Winwood concert in Fort Worth. They both had their dates. I was going solo, which was okay with me, less complicated. The concert was amazing. People were actually dancing in the aisles, me included. When the concert was over, all the gang decided to go to a bar in West Fort Worth on White Settlement Road to hang out. I left my car at Lynette's condo on Eagle Mountain Lake because I was spending the night after our evening, so I said, "Sure let's go!" So off to Pete's Trailer Park we went. When we got there we saw that there was a great band playing. We all were drinking our favorite beverages and all the girls were dancing with their beaus, but I had no one to dance with. I was watching a group of young African Americans dancing and having so much fun! I love a great dancing man and this group was amazing. So next song, I saw that they were not dancing. I had picked out one of the guys in that group to dance with. Well, being the non-introvert that I am, I tapped on this guy's shoulder and asked him if he would like to dance with me. Next thing I know, I am laid out on the floor with blood dripping out of my mouth and nose. My friends are all over me. Turns out that the people are hollering to the bar to call 911 to report an assault.

Lynette is screaming to the bar to bring us some ice, and I later found out that the guy I asked to dance had grabbed his girlfriend and whisked her out of there. My friends told me later that the girlfriend of the guy I asked to dance whacked me in the face with her fist when she heard me ask her boyfriend to dance. Thanks to Lynette and Pammy's quick responses, they got me in their car to take me to Lynette's house to nurse me. She had a stash of Lortab and I took one when I got there and kept asking them if I should go to the ER because the gash in my lower mouth was huge. I thought I might need stitches but we all decided it was okay. I spent the night at Lynette's and went back to my apartment the next day. I was hung over and still concerned about my swollen lip. By then it had become pretty swollen. "What was I going to tell my kids?" was my main concern. Lynette saw me off to Dallas from her condo and told me to just lay low for a while. So I did. I went to Wendy's twice a day and had a Frostie. I kept putting my kids off so they wouldn't see me in that shape. I was so ashamed! Eventually, I healed enough to see them and never let them know what happened to me. But eventually they found out!

During this time, I was now president of the American Singles Golf Association. Two weeks after the bar incident, we had a golfing event at Mansfield National. I had to show up. I told my partners in crime, Pammy and Lynette, that I would just tell everyone the truth. So on the morning of golf, everyone was asking me what happened to my swollen mouth. I just told them that I got whacked by this black girl in a bar because I asked her boyfriend to dance. This was perfect because they all blew me off. Yeah, sure! HA-HA! A total ruse! I'm not proud of this, but being the goodie-two-shoes as I was growing up, this was kind of a fun adventure for me to tell. It makes my mother boil but I know that there is nothing that happens to me that is not part of the plan. I have to say that having this happen to me made me so much more tolerant of the bad things that happen to people ... it is not all self-induced.

During this time I decided to run a marathon! I picked the Rock 'n' Roll marathon in San Diego in June. My future son-in-law, Greg, was living with James, Johnny and me in Arlington at the time. He had run in several marathons. He told me that he would be my trainer. So I started training to run the marathon. This was very cathartic for me to shed the pain and grief of the Duyane breakup. I would work three 12-hour shifts a week and on the other four days I was running, running and running. The training to run a first marathon was more grueling than the actual race! When I got to where I could run four hours at a time, my coach, Greg, told me that I was ready. In June of 2003 I flew to San Diego to run in the Rock 'n' Roll Marathon. I rented a Mustang convertible once again. I totally enjoyed the wonderful San Diego weather. I was told that after the marathon was done to go out and eat a great big meal. Afterwards, go back to my hotel and fill up my tub with ice water and soak in it to help with the pain.

In the very early morning hours of "the day," there was fog everywhere. You couldn't see your hand in front of your face. The locals told me it was called the "June Gloom." I heard the starting gunshot, the race began and I took off. What was so fun about this marathon was about every half a mile they had bands set up to entertain and encourage you to keep going! When I came to the half marathon point, I thought about taking that route and just do a half marathon, but I kept going. I was about to die when I reached the mile out from the finish line. With only 1.7 miles left, I was getting so weak and about to give up. This white-headed lady passed me and said, "DON'T GIVE UP NOW!" I looked at her and thought if she, being so much older than I, can finish, I am going to do it! So into one of the finish lines I headed and raised my arms to signify that I made it! As I was running down the finish lane, I saw this big sign held up that says, "Way to go KAY!!" I looked and saw that it was Lisa, her girlfriend and a guy friend of hers from Belmont University! I was so excited and surprised because she had never told me she would be there! I collapsed in her arms and told them I was starving! We headed to the old district of San Diego and had a wonderful dinner. I loved seeing her and her friends there. We had a wonderful meal and great conversation. I was worn out and needed to get back to the motel. I filled up my tub with ice and water and soaked as long as I could take it. The next day I was so sore and taking lots of Tylenol. Lisa went back to Nashville and I headed back to Dallas. I never really ran that much again after that because it was so much wear and tear on my body! But I can always say, "I finished a marathon!"

All during my single years and fiascos, there was good and bad. Johnny told me I needed to sign up for Match.com. Of course I didn't have any idea what that was. He and I sat down, got on the computer and created my profile, etc. The next day I was answering all these responses. This was a truly hit-and-miss strategy, because I kissed a lot of frogs before I found my prince, which was years later. What I loved about it was I could list on my profile that I only wanted to meet men who were believers in Jesus Christ, were golfers and had jobs with flexible hours. In other words, they could travel like I could to play golf. I sure didn't want to meet anyone in a bar, who had a motorcycle or a boat or was a big hunter. All that was totally out. This all started at the end of 2003. I met many men and hardly had two dates with anyone. My litmus test for most of the guys I met was a round of golf as a first date. I figured it was public and safe and I usually had a girlfriend play with us. I came to find out you can learn a lot about a person playing golf with them. For example, how much do they cuss, do they cheat, how selfish are they, can they take golf lightly and not throw a fit when they don't hit a perfect shot, just a few of the illuminating ideas. Some of the most unequivocable saves with this strategy was with "Cheatin' Craig" at Tangle Ridge golf course. I showed up and we played seven holes. We had some decent conversation. His golf game was mediocre, which was okay. But on hole eight, we had a grandfather and his grandson playing in front of us. They were looking all over for the boy's ball. Craig saw it next to our golf cart and picked it up and put it in his pocket. The granddad comes over and asks him if he found the ball, Craig said no, and the granddad drives off. I asked him, "How do you know that the ball you just picked up wasn't the kid's ball?" He said nothing back to me.

Cheater! So on to hole nine, a par three. He hit his shot from the men's tees and his ball cleared the ravine. It landed in the bunker in front of the green. I hit my ball from the ladies' tee and it landed on the green with a long putt. We drove to the green. He hopped out of the cart to go check out his ball in the bunker. I drove the cart up to the green. As I was getting out, I looked back and see him with his back to me.

I could tell from his movements that he was fluffing up the sand around his "fried egg" to give him a better lie in the bunker. I said nothing, because at this point he was not a "match" for me. We finished the round with very little conversation. At the end of the round I told him, "I don't think this is a match for me. Thanks." This became my mantra at the end of many more dates.

Then there was "Krazy Ken" from my old high school. He saw me on Match and reached out. I was curious because I really didn't remember him from high school. He agreed to a golf double date because one of my single girlfriends had met a guy on Match also and we decided to do this together. We set up a round of golf at Coyote Ridge in Carrollton. As the round progressed, all seemed okay except that Ken seemed very jittery and edgy. We were on hole eight and my approach to the green was about 10 feet behind Cindy's ball. I asked her to mark it. From the backside of the large green, we heard Ken yelling, "You can't do that! You can't mark your ball anywhere except on the green!" I looked at her and then I looked at him and yelled back, "Yes, you can!" He said he was going to give me a two-stroke penalty. Great date! That was a no-brainer. We all completed the round with very little said. He wanted to take me and Cindy out to eat afterwards. When I asked Cindy about it in the bathroom, all she said was "Sure! A free meal from the asshole!" So we went out to eat. I told him afterward, "This is not a match for me." So on and on it goes! At that point I got off Match and ended up having rotator cuff surgery in November 2004. So I was out for six months. No golf and no Match.com for a while.

CHAPTER 17

FOND FAMILY RECOLLECTIONS

*The Lord is my shepherd, I shall not want. He makes
me lie down in green pastures, He leads me beside quiet
waters. He restores my soul. He guides me in the paths
of righteousness for His name's sake.*

PSALM 23:1-3

To my kids, Breckenridge was like my Throckmorton. It was a
place of love and grounding. Despite all the craziness that was
our lives, they always had the steadiness and stability of my
parents and my grandmother. Since we only lived about three
hours from Breckenridge, it was a trip we could easily make
at least once a month, which we usually did.

In the early years of my marriage to John and when Lisa
and Christy were young, my parents had a beautiful house in
the town of Breckenridge. The girls loved going there because
they not only loved Mama's cooking but they loved the pool
out back! I can remember when Lisa was just 3 or 4 years old

and the kids would be in the pool, and all of us adults were sitting around sort of watching them but really talking and laughing. Lisa would shout out, "Papa, watch me!" He would take a glance but then go back to telling his stories. Then Lisa would holler, "Papa, watch and KEEP ON WATCHING!" Of course that got his attention. She never lived that saying down. On one of the trips from Plano to Breckenridge, the girls were young and sitting in the back seat. We were driving through Bridgeport, and I saw the flashing lights behind me. I pulled over and rolled down my window. "Ma'am, is there any reason that you are going over the speed limit?" Before I could say anything, Lisa stuck her little head over my shoulder and looked out the window to say, "Yes sir, we are going to Mama and Papa's house!" After that all I got was a smile and a warning from the sweet officer. When we would get close to Breckenridge, they were looking for the 10-story First National Bank Building. They knew we were close. This reminded me of Throckmorton and driving there from so many places when I was a kid. We would make that 12- to 13-hour trip from Jackson, Mississippi, or wherever we were living at the time. As we would climb the hill on the south end of Throckmorton, my siblings and I would lean over the seat to see the glistening night lights of the sleeping little town below where our grandparents lived. We would all yell, "I saw Throckmorton first!" What great memories from kids who lived in so many places. This is what Throckmorton means to me. It is still important to me because not only are my grandparents and dad buried there but also my youngest son, James. And when the time comes, my mom will be there as well as me and my husband, ML.

It was in Breckenridge that we could all know that Mom was always in the kitchen and Dad either at his office in downtown Breckenridge, playing or practicing his golf or out messing with his cows. Lots of room for the kids to roam. There was a golf cart there that taught all the kids how to drive. Just like in any small town, there was always something going on. Sometimes there were parades, which the kids participated in. How much we all loved to go out and eat at Ernie's, the local Mexican joint, where you always ran into people you knew. There was a morning tradition in my family of slurping coffee and talking long enough to solve all the world's problems. It used to be in Throckmorton around Grandma's kitchen table. It was there that my granddad taught me how to cool off my coffee if the milk hadn't fixed it. He told me to take my saucer and pour a small amount of coffee into it and then raise the saucer up to my mouth and gently blow on it, then slurp it down! I thought I was such a big girl and did it until I discovered mugs. Bye-bye cup and saucer!

After living in town since 1977, Dad finally bought the ranch he always wanted. It was about five miles south of town and was called the Gunsolus Creek Ranch. It was always called the "Place" by my kids. They built a beautiful home on the bank of the Gunsolus Creek just beyond their huge back patio. Mom and Dad built a small "library" in their house which we justly called it. It really was like a wide hallway with a large built-in bookshelf and large bay window across from the shelf. There were two large cushioned chairs with a table and a lamp in between them. Across those were two hardback chairs. This is the room where Mom and Dad would do their morning reading and coffee drinking when it was too hot or too cold to go out on the back patio overlooking the creek. It was here they would solve all of their kids' and grandkids' problems. Whenever we were there, depending on who all came, there would always be four people in there, but oftentimes you would have up to eight with babies sitting on our laps. Just drinking coffee and talking until 10 in the morning or longer. This was a place for serious conversations, crying conversations and confrontational ones too. There was much laughter and lots of talk about politics as well. Our holidays at the "Place" had so much music because James would play his guitar, Mom would play her autoharp and my brother Russell would play piano or his dulcimer. There have been times when we would have friends over and there would also be violins and bass fiddles added to the other instruments. So music was pretty basic for our get-togethers. During the holidays we would have up to nine kids and eight adults. In the early days, Dad would buy blow-up mattresses for the kids to spread through the very large family room. Like a big slumber party. Later on, Dad had a metal "casita" built just about 50 yards from the big house. Then the kids had their own place to sleep and hang out.

The "casita" became the home for my Grandma Whitaker to live in when she could no longer live in Throckmorton alone, after my granddad had died in 1978. She was very well taken care of there. She would be at all of our holiday celebrations. Since she had become totally blind and was very hard of hearing, she would just sit on a chair in the kitchen and look straight ahead. We would all, at one time or another, go over to hug and love on her. One time I was taking videos of all the action in Mom's kitchen. I looked over and saw

Grandma sitting in her kitchen chair looking straight ahead. I said, "Hey, Grandma, smile for the video." She didn't even move. Then I realized she didn't hear me, so I proceeded to yell it so loud that she jerked and suddenly smiled. I got it all on video. It was hilarious to watch her and listen to me yelling at her. The one great-grandkid that she loved the most was James because he always paid attention to her. He didn't ignore her and certainly wasn't afraid of her. From the time he was young enough to be around Grandma he loved her. He was especially fascinated with her nose. Or lack thereof. She was in her seventies when she had to have her nose totally removed due to so much tissue being scraped off from skin cancer. They made a really nice prosthetic nose for her, which she put on every day but took off at night. When James was around four, he snuck into Grandma's room to give her a kiss goodnight. He saw her with no nose and he started to panic. He ran into the kitchen yelling, "Grandma's so ugly, she has no nose!" I tried to explain it to him, but I really don't think he understood until later. James thought Grandma was funny. He would always sneak up on her because he knew she couldn't see him or hear him, but she always knew it was him. She would reach out and grab him really fast and give him a big bear hug. He would love it and laugh so hard.

Mom was in the kitchen all the time. As in all great kitchens, it was a gathering place. While she cooked, we would help out. In fact, one day Mom told James that she wondered what she would have done if she had ever gotten a job. His response was typical James, "Ah, Mama, your job has always been to cook and love everybody!" My mom realized right then and there that James had found her calling!

There were summers when the kids would spend a week with Mom and Dad. They rode horses and would go to the Breckenridge city pool to swim with some of their friends. They loved to go to Papa's office on the top floor of the First National Bank Building, 10 stories high. There they would color with all of Dad's colored pencils. Being a geologist, he had a ton of colored writing tools and lots of paper. They would take trips with Mom to Abilene for a movie or to Graham to go shopping.

My mom was quite the shopper. Lisa and Christy still love shopping with her.

During some of those summers, my son James and a couple of my nieces were out there together running wild and free.

Early on in their years in Breckenridge, my parents had started a small church called the Cornerstone where a group of believers from some of the local denominational churches started coming to on Friday nights. My mom would lead the worship and they usually had some really good speakers come. Orlando Reyes and his wife Joanne, from my TCU days, would come very often. In fact, they got to be very good friends with Mom and Dad. I'm sure Mom and Dad kept them informed of all that was going on in my life since I had left TCU. In fact, in the last 10 years I have reconnected with them, which has been a true blessing. There were a lot of miracles and answers to a lot of prayers at the Cornerstone. On our visits to Breckenridge, we would always go to the Cornerstone and the girls loved it. So in the midst of all the turmoil that went on from 1976 to 2000, there was always Breckenridge.

I need to give a tribute to my dad at this point. I've had many experiences in life with my dad. He has protected me from murder, kidnapping, extortion, some cruel people. He has shown up and been the answer. I would pray often for Jesus to show up and many times He would show up as my dad. I never asked for this, but Jesus did it in a very subtle way. I've learned that you never know how Jesus is going to show up. It could be through your best friend or your worst enemy. My dad died in 2013, and after living out there alone Mom decided to sell the ranch and move to Frisco to be closer to all her kids, grandkids and now great-grandkids. I'm just so grateful for the blessing of parents so loving, kind and always there for their kids.

During this same phase, when James was around four, he was totally enamored with the firemen near our home on Piedra Drive. The firehouse was one block from our house. So every week, James wanted to walk to the fire station and visit "the guys." When we were there, they let him put on the hat and the boots. They would put him up in the fire truck to see the instrument panels and all the equipment. It was during this same time frame that John had to call 911 for an accident I had. The firemen totally recognized James as they were helping me and taking me to the hospital.

It was a morning in 1989. The girls were already off to school and the boys and I were getting ready to go to our church where we were involved in a group called MOPS. This was basically a support group for moms with preschoolers at home. It provided a venue for getting out of the house and sharing with other moms about the life of a stay-at-home mom. I loved it. We shared recipes, child-rearing tips and just encouraged each other. The boys had so much fun in their classrooms too. I think at this point I was the only stay-at-home mom on my block. My neighbor, Katie, had two daughters in daycare. She had a great job at Club Corp as an executive secretary. Some days she would call me up and my home would be packed with neighbor kids. Our big backyard became the after-school playground. I asked her, "What's up, Katie?" In the midst of yelling, "Hey you guys, quit jumping on the sofa!" She would say, "My boss is out of town, so I'm just sitting here ordering some stuff from my catalogues." I would say, "Well, Katie, I've got to go before they tear up my house!" Ah, the life of a stay-at-home mom!

There had been a light spring shower, so the sidewalk was wet. I had the Suburban out front to load the kids into. I had on a brand-new Liz Claiborne sweater, new Liz flats and was so excited to go to MOPS. I was doing a presentation at MOPS that morning, so I was loading more into my vehicle than a normal MOPS morning. As usual, we were running behind, so I was rushing around. As I walked down the sidewalk and made a small right turn to go to the Suburban, my right foot slipped out from under me and I caught myself in the fall with my right arm. When I landed, I could hear a snap and I was screaming bloody murder. I knew I was in bad trouble. I was screaming so much that Johnny, who saw it all, ran into the house and told his dad, "Hey, Dad, I think Mom just had a heart attack!" So John ran outside and saw me splayed out on the sidewalk screaming. He called 911 and the good ol' firemen came to my rescue. I was totally out of it in tremendous pain as James watched his heroes help his mom. They started me out with some nitrous oxide to ease the pain and then proceeded to cut off my new jacket and sweater. I was yelling, "Please don't cut up my new sweater and jacket." They were like, "Ma'am, we have to look at your arm." I acquiesced and gave up because what did that matter anyway? I was in so much pain, way more severe than during any childbirth. I can remember on the drive to Plano General Hospital they would put the inhaler over my nose to administer the nitrous oxide and shortly after getting a dose I was begging for more. The Pain. Oh my!

Once we got to the ER, I was frantic! I knew that a friend of mine from high school was an orthopedic doctor there. I kept yelling that I wanted Brad Britt to take care of me. Please call him! They did and Brad showed up. He was amazing. My pain was subsiding from the Demerol they gave me. I had all the X-rays done and he came in, gave me and John the diagnosis and prognosis. It was really bad. The head of my radius was severely shattered in the fall. I had the tiny fragments of the scattered bone throughout my bicep muscle. This was causing all the pain. He said I needed surgery right away. So they took me to surgery and Brad took care of me. Post-op, he came to me and said that it was so much worse than he thought. It took him hours to pick all the bone fragments out. He said since my radial head was missing he had to put in an artificial piece to replicate the radial head. I went home several days later to heal. I was in a cast for quite a while. He told me that I would need another surgery to remove the implant and get my elbow fixed. He sent me to Dr. Buzz Burkhead at Carrell Clinic. When I went to see him, he said he could fix my elbow. So more surgery. This time he said he would connect one of my elbow muscles to help my elbow do the rotation that I had lost. I couldn't open a door or bring a fork to my mouth with my right arm. I learned to do a lot with my left arm. I went in for another surgery and he said he believed that it was fixed. I now just needed to heal and get into a lot of physical therapy. Which I did. I ended up with a passive motion machine for my elbow at the house. I had home health care and they would monitor my progress.

Can you see the scene? I had this Terminator device on my right arm when I wasn't on the machine. I had to be on the machine, sitting and letting the machine move and rotate my elbow for six hours a day. This was no small feat for a mom with four children and a husband who was not exactly supportive. I really depended on my daughters to get us through this. Plus, my MOPS friends were there for me and my family. There was a chain of meals that just kept coming. I did this for four months and there was no progress. I kept telling Doc Buzz that something was not right. He ordered an X-ray and he came to the room with the bad news. He said that because of the severity of the injury the bone in my radius had decided to create more bone cells. He called it "heterotopic" bone tissue. He explained it this way ... "The bones down from the elbow are the ulna and the radius. They have to be able to rotate around each other for us to use a fork and open a door. Well, the new bone tissue had grown and fused the ulna and the radius together so there was no movement possible without another surgery to get rid of the bone and release the ulna and radius." I was beside myself. I asked him if he could do this surgery and he told me that he didn't want to do it. He was going to send me to the Mayo Clinic in Rochester, Minnesota. I told him that I would live with my arm the way it was for a while because my marriage was deteriorating. I needed a break. He said that would be fine if I needed a break. So I learned how do most everything with my left arm ... eating, opening doors, etc. In the meantime, the marriage was going down the tubes and I also believed that John was having some problems at work with some disgruntled clients coming after him for lying to them. In 1992 after our divorce was final, I decided to go to the Mayo Clinic and have the surgery. In May 1993 my dad accompanied me to Rochester, Minnesota and my mom stayed with the kids in Plano. We checked into the hospital. I met the renowned Dr. Bernard Morrey. He had previously been an engineer for General Dynamics in Fort Worth. He changed careers and became a prominent orthopedic surgeon to help all elbow issues. I certainly had issues! I got checked in and Dad went off to play golf. This was his ulterior motive to being my escort instead of Mom, but as a golfer now I don't blame him. I would have done the same thing. No use sitting alone in a sterile hospital waiting room when adventure awaits you on the beautiful golf courses of Minnesota. I went into surgery and I remember coming out and finding the passive motion machine connected to my right elbow. Dr. Morrey came in and told me, "All is well, I have fixed your elbow. You will be fine. I don't see that you will even need therapy after you leave here." I was so grateful I cried. Just like he said, when I got home I never went to therapy. To this day that elbow is working fine and I can use a fork with my right hand.

I was there for about three more days, enough time to give Dad some good golfing experiences. When he picked me up from the hospital, I asked him to take me across the state line to Wisconsin. I told him that I wanted to see the Little House on the Prairie Museum. While homeschooling the girls, one of our best projects was building the cabin and doing a dress-up enactment of the Laura Ingalls Wilder books scenario. We read a lot when I was homeschooling. So many precious times. I read *Little Women, Silver Skates, Anne of Green Gables, Lassie Come Home, Where the Red Fern Grows*, the Laura Ingalls Wilder series, *Pilgrim's Progress*, and a myriad more to them. To this day my daughter, Lisa, still calls me "Marmy!" Just like the *Little Women* girls called their "Marmy."

Once home from the Mayo Clinic, I was able to continue my life with a fresh start. I was going back to school to become a nurse. I was still in therapy with Rob and going to Al-Anon once a week. This whole ordeal was just a bump in the road. Moving forward now. Always forward … there is nothing the other way.

My dad had planned a trip for our family to go to the island of Nevis the next summer. It was winter of 1994 and I was doing great physically and in nursing school. The only one of my kids who could go was Lisa. Christy was off at ski camp with her church youth group and the boys were snowboarding with their dad. We were so excited to do this. My brother, Russell, and his two kids went. Also my sister, Cheryl, and my brother-in-law, Bob, with their three little girls. It was our first big family trip. Off we headed to St. Kitts in the Caribbean. From there we took a two-hour boat ride to the island of Nevis. It was a dream come true. I was pretty free since my daughter was about 14 at the time. She really didn't need much chaperoning. She helped my sister with her young girls around the pool. The guys were all playing golf at the beautiful course which was a part of the Nevis Four Seasons Resort. One day I asked Dad if I could ride on the golf cart with him when they played golf. I was always a big tennis player and always thought that golf seemed pretty boring and an old man's game. Since my arm situation had drastically ended my tennis days, my dad told me I should take up golf because in golf your right arm can be your enemy. So I went up the mountain to watch these three men conquer the course. My takeaway from this outing was that the most beautiful places on the earth must be on golf courses, not sitting around the pool babysitting the little ones. I was hooked. I told Dad I wanted to play golf. He got me a lesson with the Nevis pro. I rented some clubs and played a round with the big boys. I was terrible but I was hooked.

While we were there, Dad was always complaining about the price of everything. Because Nevis is not a self-sustaining country, all their produce had to be imported, thus the prices reflected that. Very expensive tomatoes and strawberries. We left the resort one night to eat at a local restaurant. When we walked in we saw this old drunken guy leaning over the bar. Dad said, "Hey, check out the guy at the bar! I just heard that last year he brought his family to Nevis and he lost everything because of it!" Of course we all are thinking, "Hilarious, Papa!" We never returned, but for all of us who went, we had a blast and I became a golf lover. It was during this time that I had met Duyane and we were in early dating stages. I wrote to him from Nevis and told him that I had played golf and loved it. When I got back, he had bought me a used set of Jack Nicklaus women's golf clubs. So we started playing golf together. He taught me how to navigate a golf course and about the game itself. I was in for the long haul.

CHAPTER 18

THROCKMORTON GAL

My delight is in the law of the Lord and in His law I meditate day and night. I am like a tree firmly planted by streams of water, which yields its fruit in its season, and its leaf does not wither; and whatever I do I prosper.

PSALM 1:1-3

Throckmorton

My husband ML has always told people that I am an "old Throckmorton girl." I usually have to clarify and let them know that I was not from Throckmorton, but felt like I should be. Throckmorton was a small North Central Texas town just a 45-minute drive north of Breckenridge. It's where my dad grew up and met my mom in eighth grade. They got married there. It was where we always called home when the oil patch kept calling us to far and distant places. It was also the home to the famous Dallas Cowboys football player, Bob Lilly. My mom actually was his babysitter when she was around 13 and he was only four. She loves to tell the story of how the big and strong Bob Lilly was so easily scared into crying by my mom when she would chase him around the house with his mother's fox stole.

My first horse story that I can remember happened in Throckmorton when I was around 10 years old. I was at my friend Debbie's house and we decided to get her Shetland pony saddled up and ride him. I wasn't the most savvy horse person but the Shetland was tiny and cute. Things started out okay but then this cute pony panicked and took off into a cactus patch. Once we were in there he went berserk. Started kicking and raising up. Well, needless to say, I fell off right into the middle of this cactus patch. I screamed and Debbie went and got her mom and dad. Her dad got me out of the patch. I was crying and hurting. The rest of our playtime was spent with me turned over Debbie's mom's knee as she was using her tweezers to get all the cactus stickers out of my rear end. I never really was much of a horse fan after that.

Another scary Throckmorton event happened around my junior year in high school. In a small Texas town there is not a lot to do to entertain teens during the summer. The one thing they could do was drive up and down the main road through town and check out anyone else who was cruising. I had made some really good friends since coming to Throckmorton all these years. So it was a Friday night and I asked my grandparents if I could go riding with the girls. They were pretty loose with me and said, "Sure, just be safe!" The girls came and got me and off we go cruising. After a while a couple of the guys stopped us and wanted us to go "spotlighting" with them. I didn't know what this was … so they explained it to me. We got into Floy's car with Randy. The car was a two-door Chevy Chevelle. I got into the back seat with Randy and another girlfriend and the other one was sitting up front with Floy. We proceeded to some backroads on the southwest side of Throckmorton and headed down some caliche roads spotlighting, looking for "whatever." It was starting to get late and I said, "I really need to head back home." Floy gunned his car and we headed back down the caliche road. He saw a left turn in the road ahead and slammed on his brakes. When you do this on caliche, you slide forever. Next thing I know I feel like I am in a washing machine tumbling inside of the car all over my friends. It was bizarre! The car was tumbling and rolling. Once it finally stopped, there was total silence. We were right side up when we stopped rolling, thankfully. Floy quietly asked, "Is everyone okay?" We all responded, "Okay!" No one could really move, especially those of us in the back seat where Randy, who was a big guy, was in an unusual position. Our windows had all been rolled up because of the dust off the caliche road. Floy couldn't open the doors in the front and the back seat didn't have a door, only the small triangular window. He asked me if I could roll down the back seat window and crawl out. I said, "I'll try." I reached down and thank the Lord I could roll it down. I crawled out and was able to open the passenger side door and eventually everyone got out of the car.

Silence.

We were in a little shock I'm guessing, looking back. Floy was looking around his car to see how bad the damage was and he was shocked at how it came out pretty much unscathed. After he checked his car out, Randy was looking around to see where we ended up. He went about 50 yards from where we landed and asked, "Hey, you guys, come over here and check this out." We all walked slowly toward Randy who had the spotlight turned on. Then we saw what he wanted us to see. Right in front of us was a big drop-off to a pile of big rocks below. We would have probably all died if we had gone off that cliff. Once again, silence. I just remember we were all making big sighing noises. All of us girls started crying. Randy and Floy started working on his car and got it started. We slowly got back into the car because we were too far out to walk back to Throckmorton. I started telling them that God saved us. "The Lord was really watching over us!" Silence.

The guys dropped us off at one of the girls' car and she drove me home to my grandparents' house. By then I was home about an hour later than I was supposed to be. When I walked in, my granddad and grandma were sitting in the living room staring at me! They were furious. I started crying and told them that I was in a car wreck. Of course they grilled me on all the details. I told them the who, what, and where of the whole saga. Needless to say, they were grateful that we were spared but my cruising days in Throckmorton became pretty much over. I'll never forget the feeling of tumbling inside that car. Fortunately I've never been in an accident like that again.

Rodeo

Because my dad grew up to be a cowboy, he took that to the big cities we lived in. Rodeos were a big entertainment for us. We would always go with my grandparents to the Stamford Cowboy Reunion when I was a young girl and before we moved to Canada. There was also the Junior Rodeo in

Throckmorton which we always went to when we were there. One year my granddad asked me if I wanted to be in it. I said I would if my cousin Cindy would be in it with me. Now, she is a real cowgirl. I wanted her to help me. Her granddad and my granddad were brothers. They were really close. So of course they were excited for Cindy to come from Henrietta to Throckmorton to rodeo with me. I rode this really tame horse my granddad owned. After much practice, I decided I was going to do the "Pole Bending and Ringers" events. It was a no-brainer. Most of the kids who entered this were under the age of 10. Cindy was a barrel racer so that was her event. We got new cowgirl outfits, hats and new boots. The most fun was riding through the middle of Throckmorton in the Junior Rodeo parade. On the day of the rodeo, I did my event and Cindy had coached me well. The rodeo was on the west side of Throckmorton at the Asharena, owned by a local rancher. A tragic thing happened toward the end of this event. They had an event called a Double Barrel Race. The big girls from high school participated in this one. There were two horses with riders. They started out from both sides of the arena and rounded their barrels then crossed by each other to do the other set of barrels. Then raced out of the arena. The one who completes this the fastest wins. We are all watching from the stands, when out comes the second to the last contestants. Cindy was one of the last contestants. As they were completing their first round of barrels and they headed to the other set, the horses had a head-on collision with each other. The girls were knocked off their horses. They got up and saw how badly hurt both of the horses were. The stands were totally silent. No one could believe what had just happened. The average speed a horse travels in a barrel race as he goes to the first set of barrels and exits after rounding the last set is about 20 miles per hour. So when those horses rammed breast-on into each other there was a tremendous amount of power. They both ended up with broken necks and had to be put down after they were taken out of the arena. Cindy never got to do her race because she was one of the last contestants. As we were walking to get our horses and leave, there was very little talk. People were just shocked that they had witnessed such a tragedy.

Once we moved to Calgary, the rodeoing continued. The famous Calgary Stampede became our way to remember Texas. They had the regular rodeo events like in Texas but Albertans added another event for which Calgary became famous. It was the famous "Chuckwagon Races." It was a very high-energy event with chuckwagons racing around a track led by four thoroughbred horses. This is now a rodeo sport in most of the large rodeos around this country. To make the rodeo experience part of our home life, Dad bought us a house out in the country, where he proceeded to buy a horse, which he rode almost every day after work. This is when I think my little sister started her lifelong love of horses. We also had two big dogs and would catch prairie dogs in the big field behind our house. I guess the old saying "You can take the boy out of Texas but you can't take Texas out of the boy" stuck with my dad.

When I was at TCU, every year my granddad came from Throckmorton to sell and buy cattle at the Fort Worth Stock Show. He always took me to the Rodeo. I loved it. He would pick me up at my dorm and we would go to Cattlemen's

Steakhouse down in the Stockyards and eat a great steak with all the trimmings. A couple of times he took me to the Cattlemen's Ball at the Blackstone Hotel in downtown Fort Worth. We would dance and he would mingle with all his cowboy buddies. Then later on when I had kids and my parents had their ranch in Breckenridge, my dad picked up the mantle and every year for decades he would buy 20 seats for the Stock Show. This was a really big deal for my kids and our cousins. We kept going up until 2010.

When we lived in Houston, we would go to the Houston Livestock Show and Rodeo. This was where I got to see "The King!" But the most unusual rodeo Dad would ever take us to was the Huntsville Prison Rodeo in Huntsville, Texas. This would take place every October. The inmates had to try out for the many rodeo events that were held. We would sit in the grandstands and look across the arena. Behind a large barbed wire fence sat the inmate trustees all dressed in white jumpsuits with armed guards everywhere. One year we had seats next to the inmates with the barbed fence separating us. I remember looking at those inmates and wondering why they were there. What had they done? The inmates who got to be in the rodeo all wore large striped shirts like prison inmates wore back in the day.

CHAPTER 19

UNKNOWN JAMES

*I waited patiently for the Lord; And He inclined to me
and heard my cry. He brought me up out of the pit of
destruction, out of the miry clay; and He set my feet upon a
rock, making my footsteps firm. And He put a new song
in my mouth, a song of praise to my God; many will see
and fear, And will trust the Lord. Since I am afflicted and
needy, let the Lord be mindful of me. Thou art my help and
Deliverer: Do not delay, O my God.*

PSALM 40:1-3, 17

*Weeping may last for the night,
but a shout of joy comes in the morning.*

PSALM 30:5

James was my youngest child. He was born in Breckenridge, Texas, on September 30, 1986. It was his favorite town in the world. As he grew up, he loved my mom and dad and their ranch. I used to always tell James that he should have been born in 1885 when my great-grandma, "Ma Whitaker," was riding on the cattle trails from Abilene to Kansas. He would have been a perfect fit for that lifestyle. Unfortunately, that is not what he was destined to be on this earth. He was destined to a schooling that defied his creative juices and depressed his off-the-wall ideas. James was, as my dad said, "A shooting star that ran out." James was the kid who could watch a movie, let's say, *Wizard of Oz*, and do a recital from the part of the script where Dorothy meets the Tin Man, the Lion and the Scarecrow to all of them meeting the Grand Wizard! He would sing all the songs and he had the script down! At four years old! His whole childhood was full of imagination. I can't even think of a character he didn't imitate. I made a costume for *Ghostbusters, Knights in Shining Armor, Cowboys,* and many more. He not only loved the costumes, he had dialogue to go with each, either directly from a movie or from his own creation. He entertained our whole family for 23 years. James was playing a small guitar at age three and singing a lot. One of his favorite songs to sing for us when he three was "Do Wah Diddy Diddy." He was such a character who would entertain and make us all laugh. Once we moved to Arlington and left Plano, he really blossomed in his musical talent. His buddies, the Bothe boys, were always at either our home or he was down at theirs. I can remember James would sit on the curb of our cul-de-sac, play his guitar and sing for anyone to hear. It wasn't until later on that I realized how much that meant to some of our neighbors. He was just the kind of human being who loved people and in most settings he was irresistible to love.

One day I came home from work and I heard someone playing our piano. The only person in our family who ever played the piano was me or Lisa, but I knew she was at Belmont University. James was around 14. I walked into the living room and was shocked! I said, "James, what are you doing?" He just looked up from the keyboard and said, "Playing the piano, duh!" I asked him when he learned to play the piano, and he said he just sat down and started playing. I asked, "Would you like me to find you a piano teacher?" He said, "No, Mom, but thanks." Then he proceeded to keep playing some beautiful chords and I realized that this kid didn't need a teacher, like I did. He had the music in him and it was all by ear. He started to excel in all his music. He could play anything he wanted on any guitar. My brother had let him use some of his fancy electric guitars and James excelled. His piano playing got better and better the more he played. With all this success with music, it was so hard to see him have so many struggles with the other areas of his life. It wasn't until he was around 16 that I realized how bad it was getting. But I didn't think it was struggling at this time. I just thought it was teenage rebellion. It was way more than that, but I didn't see it at that point.

In 2003, James was struggling with school. He was not able to keep up with the rigors of school. He basically just wasn't showing up for class. I kept getting notices that he wasn't there. He was a sophomore at that time. I was single and working three 12-hour shifts a week. I was really struggling with James' out-of-control behavior. He started staying out late with buddies and had a few drunken episodes that I witnessed. It was like there was nothing I could say or do to get him to act rationally. I even at one point called my parents and wanted to take him to Breckenridge so we could all talk to him. He was heading down a huge hole.

So off James and I went to see Mama and Papa. He had no idea what the purpose of the trip was. That first night, we were all sitting out on the back patio and Dad started to talk. He basically told James that they knew all the trouble he was getting into and not showing up for class. James started to argue with the three of us and my dad got so angry. He told James to go in the house. After James left, I asked Dad what was he going to do. Dad replied, "I think that boy needs a good whupping!" I was stunned. So Mom and I looked at each other as Dad got up to go inside. We waited for a while and Dad returned without James. "Did James cry, Dad?" "Nope, he didn't! And I don't know what to tell you, Sweetie, but I think it is time for you to hand him over to his dad, because this is getting to be more than you can handle."

Johnny was living with us and so was my future son-in-law, Greg. During this struggling period there was lots of arguing between James and each one of us, me, Johnny and Greg. It was time for the changes to start. I spoke with his dad and he was willing to take James in to live with them. I thought this would be good for him because he and his brother Johnny were fighting about their dad a lot, and this might be a good move to help James figure out who his dad really was.

So during the end of the school year, John let James move in with him, his new wife and their young son, Josh. Greg and my daughter Christy had gotten married, so he was out of the house. Johnny had already moved out and was living with some buddies in Plano. Before he left Arlington, James and I went to Plano to check out several private schools that would help him graduate from high school, since he was so behind in almost every subject except creative music. We found a small private school in Plano that had a self-advancement program.

I never felt good about this change but I really didn't have a lot of choices. I was still going to my counselor, Rob, and he was encouraging me in my decisions. It was one baby step after another trying to help James. I basically just let go of James and placed him in John Apple's care.

James was doing the best he could with the school he was in and he did graduate in January 2005. His buddies from Arlington all came to his graduation at Willow Bend Academy. He barely got through. When he was going to Willow Bend, he loved going over to my sister Cheryl's house and playing her grand piano. After he got out of school, he was just "Helter Skelter" as far as living life. He went through a lot, living with his dad. In 2008, his dad's home was raided by the FBI with police all over the street and helicopters hovering over their home and street. They took all his computers and files. The sky was falling for John Apple and James was there to see it. John was not arrested at that time. In January 2012, he pleaded guilty to two charges, one count of security fraud and one count of conspiracy to commit securities fraud. In April 2012, he was sentenced to 10 years in prison and restitution of $53 million. James wasn't around to see any of this except the raid. John eventually died in prison in October 2015. After the 2008 raid, James moved out of his dad's house and moved in with a girlfriend he had from high school, Crystal. They had a very tumultuous relationship. James was crazy about her and I truly believe Crystal loved him, but his insanity was getting to her. It made living with him very unpredictable. It ended and not surprisingly, they split up. During all these episodes, James wasn't able to get a steady job. The only kind of job he kept for any time was making smoothies at Smoothie King or a health food store in Frisco. The other thing that James would do when not making smoothies was go to the Steinway store in Frisco and play their pianos. They loved to see him come into the store.

He couldn't operate in this world. He didn't come around the family very much during that period, because when he did we all would try to talk to him about life and moving forward with his own life. He would always argue with each of us. We would all shake our heads and wonder, "What is he thinking?" After a few years he decided he wanted to go live with my brother, Russ, in Irving for a while. Russ and James had always spent a lot of time together playing their instruments and making music. They were very entertaining for our whole clan when we would all get together at my parents' ranch in Breckenridge. Russ recognized the talent that James had and would try to get James to learn to play popular songs. James had other plans. Wesley, James' favorite cousin, was going to Vanderbilt in Nashville, Tennessee. James and Wes were very close and were both great musicians. So in December of 2005, James drove his beat-up car to Nashville and landed at Wes' apartment front door. He told him he was going to get a job and live with him! While he was staying with Wes, I would call him every other day or so to see if he had gotten a job. Always no. I told him he should go to the studios on Music Row and audition for a guitar playing position.

Not happening.

It was December 2005 and he had been at Wes' a few days with no job prospects, and no apparent incentive either. I was getting impatient with his inability to move forward.

One morning, when I was off work, I got a call from Wesley. He was panicked and scared and told me that James had been admitted to the psyche ward at Vanderbilt University Hospital. I was stunned! I actually became immobile for a minute but then my innate survivor instincts kicked in. He told me the whole story of how James was home in Wes' apartment. When Wes came home from class, James was sitting on the kitchen floor with a kitchen knife to his throat telling Wes, "They are coming to get us!" Wes said he talked him out of the knife and drove him to the Vanderbilt ER. I called my dad's secretary and told her what was going on. "Judy, will you please make me a reservation on Southwest to get me to Nashville as soon as possible?" She said she would and then told my dad. I called him and told him what had happened at Wesley's apartment and that I needed to get to Nashville. He totally agreed. When I arrived In Nashville, I headed to see Wes. We immediately went to the psyche ward to see James. They led me to his room. He was a torn-up emotional wreck. As soon as he saw me, he was bawling and begging me to get him out of there. I was more cautious and told him we needed to see what the doctor said about what had happened to him. I asked him if they were giving him meds and he said yes, but he was hiding them under his tongue and spitting them out after the nurse left the room. Finally, I got to meet his doctor. He was an Indian and right off the bat I got the impression that he didn't want to deal with a woman. I told him that I was a nurse and we lived in Texas. I also told him that I really wanted to take James back to Texas where all his family lived. I told him that I had a place for James at La Hacienda in Kerrville, because we all were thinking that drugs were involved in his bizarre behavior. The doctor was getting red in the face and told me that he wasn't releasing James to me because he didn't think he was ready to leave. I was okay with that. I told him I would be back every day to check on him, since I had gotten a hotel room. He pointed his finger to the door and told me to get out and that I couldn't see James for a week. I was not allowed to come onto the floor at any time. I was devastated and very confused at his abruptness. I kissed James goodbye and told him I was praying and would be back to get him whenever the doctor released him. I told James to do everything the doctor and nurses told him to do, especially swallow his meds.

When I got back to the Hampton Inn, the Lord gave me the whole Psalm 40 for James. I prayed this Psalm for him every day and night. I called my girlfriend, Lynette, to see if she knew a reputable attorney in Nashville. She did and I called him that day. I told him about the events and what the doctor at the hospital had done. I gave him the name of the doctor and he said he would do some research on him and call me the next day. He called and told me that this particular psychiatrist had a terrible reputation. He also added that there was nothing else he could do to help me out. So despite all the effort, I had to wait the week out and then James was released. We flew to San Antonio from Nashville. I can remember being so scared in the airports, because I didn't know what crazy antics he would pull off or if he would run away from me. Fortunately, he was very docile for the whole trip.

Once in San Antonio, we spent the night there with no crazy events happening. The next morning, we drove to the drug rehab center, La Hacienda, in Kerrville, about a 90-minute drive. I got him checked in to La Hacienda, drove back to San Antonio and caught a plane back to Dallas. The next morning, I got a call from La Hacienda and his counselor told me that they couldn't keep James there because he wasn't a drug addict. He told me that through the night, James had been cutting himself and I needed to come and pick him up. So back on the plane to San Antonio I went to get James. I drove to Kerrville and back to the San Antonio airport then home to Dallas. During all that I was in communication with my dear counselor, Rob, to help us get through this crisis.

What do I do with James? He got James a room at the psyche ward at Richardson Medical Center. James was there for three days and then the staff decided that he was not psychotic, therefore he was not eligible to stay. James came back with me to my apartment. We went to see Rob together twice a week. Rob was giving James ultimatums that he had to get a job. James signed up for a program at my church called Barnabas Project. It was a lifestyle support group for young adults. He didn't stay with it for very long, though. I was still working three 12-hour shifts a week. I would come home and see James in the apartment or see him come strolling in after I got home from work. I would ask him what he had been doing and he said that he was walking over to the Inter-Continental Hotel off the Tollway and Belt Line Road and playing the grand piano in the foyer all day and getting tips. I was furious, although inside I'm thinking that's pretty creative, but it's not meeting the parameters. So after a couple of weeks of the same old, same old, Rob tells me and James that James should put all his belongings in a big black plastic bag and throw them into his car and leave my apartment. So James did leave and he headed back to Arlington where he was comfortable with his best buddies, the Bothe boys, who still lived on our same street with their dad. This lasted a few months. Then he moved in with his buddy Trey's family for a month or two. He was bouncing around. I think because of James' erratic behavior and wild ideas, the parents were not wanting their kids hanging out with him. He was not really going anywhere. Eventually he moved in with Tanson and Kolby in their apartment in Fort Worth off of 7th Street. All seemed to be going well for him. I would go over and take him to lunch. We would talk and he would share that he was okay. I wasn't really sure.

In 2006, I found out how nutty his life was becoming when he called me up and said that he needed to take his car into the shop to have some work done to it. I said okay and told him to have the mechanic call me when he was done. The guy called me next day and the first thing he said was, "Ma'am, have you seen your son's car lately?" I told him I had not. "Why, what is wrong with it?" He said, "Everything! I don't even know how he drives it!" He started to list everything wrong and then I asked, "Is it salvageable?" He said, "If it were my son's car I would get rid of it and not let him have another car until he can take care of one!" I told him I would greatly appreciate if he would get rid of it for me and he said he would. I really did appreciate his honesty because at this point I really didn't know how lost James was becoming.

He got a job at the Radio Shack across the street from the apartment. I could tell he didn't really like it, but he went and made a little money to help with the rent and some food. At this time, he had no car, no phone. Lisa had given him her keyboard. So when he wasn't at work, he would play the keyboard in the apartment. He also found a Steinway store about a mile from the apartment off Camp Bowie, where he would play the pianos in their basement like he had done in Dallas and Frisco. About six months later, he quit working at Radio Shack and told the boys that he was going to take the keyboard and his cowboy hat and play the keyboard on the streets of downtown Fort Worth to earn a little street change. He realized that his keyboard batteries were dead, so back he went to Radio Shack, where had just quit, and bought some new batteries. Typical James. He stayed out into the wee hours of the morning for the first night. He called me the next day. He had earned about $100 for two hours of playing on the streets. He said he was going to keep doing it. I encouraged him.

James kept playing his keyboard on the street until one fateful night when a guy stopped by to hear him play. After he sang "Don't Stop Believing" by Journey, the guy left a big tip but also said, "You think you can play this to a bunch of my customers at my bar?" "Of course," James says, "Hey man, no problem." So off he goes following this guy at around one o'clock in the morning into a basement off of Houston Street in downtown Fort Worth with his portable piano under his arm. Next thing he knows he is seated at a huge grand piano across from another huge grand piano. The crowd was drunk and unruly. Tommy, the manager and instigator, introduced

James with some huge vibrato, and said, "Who wants to hear a guy I just met on the street audition for a spot here at Pete's Dueling Piano Bar?" Well, this was a cue for an unruly crowd to go crazy. The crowd was elated and held their late-night breath to hear him play the piano. And play the piano he did, with all his passion. The late-night crowd was tremendously satisfied to accept James as the next "Piano Man" at Pete's Dueling Piano Bar.

Of course, Tommy hired James for the job that night. The only problem was that he did not know enough songs to be a Piano Bar Man. Tommy, his boss, told him that he needed to learn a total of 150 songs to be eligible to play at Pete's. This totally motivated James to go to the Steinway piano store on Camp Bowie, take his headphones which had all his songs downloaded and proceed to memorize them.

Only two years before, James' uncle Russ had asked him to do the same thing, but it was only important now to James. He studiously learned all the songs and the music. He was such a hit at Pete's. Making a lot of money. Spending it recklessly. His roommates, the Bothe boys, would tell me that he would buy very expensive guitars from Guitar Center and return them for his money back. Crystal, his ex-girlfriend, told us a Guitar Center story about James. She and James were at Guitar Center trying out guitars when this guy came out of nowhere to sample one of their guitars. All the people nearby were watching and were mesmerized at his playing, until James got hold of a guitar nearby. After he finished playing, the old guy put his guitar down and said, "I give up." Typical James!

The struggles in Fort Worth continued. I lived in Dallas, working as a nurse, and he was in Fort Worth working at Pete's. He shared with me the problems of being served the free shots as the "Piano Man." I knew that this was a problem for him, but I had no idea that there was a marijuana problem too.

CHAPTER 20

PRECIOUS PEARL

*Instead of your shame you shall have a double portion, and
instead of your humiliation they will shout for joy over their
portion. Therefore they will possess a double portion in their
land. Everlasting joy will be theirs.*

ISAIAH 61:7-8

I recovered from my shoulder surgery in April 2005 and was
ready to get back to playing golf with my friends. I also started
back on Match.com. Around February, I got a "wink" from a
guy on Match and he looked rather promising. In his profile
he stated that he was a Christian, raised a Baptist, graduated
from TCU, loved golf, especially golfing trips. Looked really good to me. I "winked" back. For a whole month we just
emailed each other, talking about our lives and jobs. Finally,
ML said, "Let's meet!" I was excited. So, of course, I asked him
to meet me for a round of golf. He agreed. I was playing that
coming Friday morning at nine on Grapevine Municipal Golf
Course with my friend, Cindy. As the day arrived, it was a

beautiful spring morning. It was May 12, 2005 and I got there around nine. I drove down to the parking lot in my Toyota Solara convertible. I had told ML what kind of car I had when he asked what I would be driving. As I parked and got out of my car, ML was right there in a golf cart next to my trunk. I popped the trunk and he got my clubs out for me and put them on the cart. I told him, "I'll just go and pay my green fee, then we can hit some balls. I see Cindy is already here." He responded, "No bother, I already took care of the green fee and I bought us some practice balls too." I was stunned. In all my Match golf dates, never has anyone done all that ML had done prior to a round of golf. I was impressed to say the least. My friend Cindy was watching and when I saw her on the driving range she gave me a thumbs up! We rode together and started talking and talking. This date was on a Friday at a municipal golf course. If you know what I'm talking about, that means the round is going to be extremely slow because the course is packed with a lot of golfers who are basically "hackers." My friend, who was in the cart ahead of us, is normally very impatient on a golf course and today was no different. We were on the third hole and ML and I were talking away waiting on the tee box and Cindy is getting very impatient and she yells, "Will you guys shut the f**k up and hit the ball!" I was shocked at her remark and told her, "Look up there, the guys in front of us are only about a hundred yards away. We can't hit yet, just chill out!" She calmed down and we kept talking. I asked him why his name was "ML." He told me that when he was a freshman at TCU and on the football team, he kept hearing the nicknames for all the varsity players. He realized that he didn't want to be just "Mike" like his high school friends called him, so he shouted out that his name was ML and it stuck. I asked him why he picked "ML" and he said because he was named after his step-grandfather, Martin Leonhard. But to this day he tells people that "ML" stands for Martin Luther. I guess you pick which Martin Luther that is. Also, to this day, whenever we go to funerals in Fort Worth and someone calls him "Mike," I know that was pre-TCU days.

This was a great beginning to a wonderful, sweet relationship. We spent a lot of time together. Lots of golf. There were times when ML would lose his temper on the course but it never made him into a grump. He would get over it and when we would get into the car to leave, he would always say, "Wasn't that a great day on the course?" I would always agree because his response was so not like the other guys, who would carry their grumpiness to whatever we did after golf, complaining about one thing or another. It was a pleasant surprise. To ML golf was "all about the swing." He was a perfectionist at his job and I could tell he was one on the course too. He would expect that each shot should be "Palmer Perfect." One day I had enough and told him, "Who do you think you are, Arnold Palmer or someone like him? You are just a regular hacker like most of us Americans. Just out here having a good time. Hopefully loving the game of golf." He was a little taken aback after that but he settled down a bit on the course. I couldn't believe I actually said that to him. This was the new me. I was not going to coddle and cover up red flags this time. I was done with that.

ML shared with me that he had resisted all of his mother's attempts to get him to say yes to Jesus. Then he told me that shortly before his mother passed away in 2005, he had

come to his senses. He had a breakdown and knew that he
needed Jesus. He had been depressed and aware that his life
was heading nowhere in his personal relationships and he
was ready for something new. He went to a counselor. She
told him about Bible Study Fellowship and suggested that he
go to learn about the Bible. He freaked out because his mom
was one of the first leaders in the DFW area to start this Bible
teaching. He started going and liked it. We met a couple of
years later. ML shared with me that he had an encounter with
the Holy Spirit in his studio one painful night and he truly
surrendered his life to the Lord. After all of this sharing, ML
asked me if I wanted us to go to church together. I never had
any of my Match dates ask me this question, so I was excited.
I told him that I was going to church with my oldest daughter
and her family to a church in Dallas called Fellowship Dallas.
This was a huge turning point in our relationship. ML was
ready and said yes. We started going and settled down for
some years at Fellowship Dallas. As it turns out, my counsel-
or, Rob, and his wife went there also. I introduced him to Rob
and we went to him for a couple of sessions of counseling to
get Rob's okay. After several years, Rob and ML became very
good friends.

He kept coming back, and in June of 2006 we decided to
get married.

Because we are big golfers, we opted for the Byron Nelson
Room at the Four Seasons Hotel in Irving as our venue. My
children were of course a little apprehensive in the beginning
of our relationship, but they warmed up to his kindness and
gentleness. My daughters, Christy and Lisa, made a comment
to my mom about ML. My mom had asked them, "What do

you all think about the guy your mom is dating?" They told her, "He looks like Moses and is very nice." Well, that really doesn't pass the test but it sounds very "kosher!" He was also very generous.

It was a sweet, small wedding. James and Lisa picked out the entertainment. They selected "God Bless The Broken Road" to sing at the wedding, which was perfect. Because God knows we had both come together from broken roads. We had a small crowd of intimate friends there who had been through all our crap over the years. More of my friends than ML's. The song they sang was perfect for us. My road was definitely broken and God blessed it with His love and grace in our lives by bringing us together. We had a wonderful honeymoon by staying in the golf course suites and playing golf both days. I loved our retreat.

Before we got married, ML lived in his studio down in the Design District of Dallas. He asked me if I wanted to live in one of the new townhomes they were building in downtown Dallas. We went to look at a few. I could never get on board. I would look out the high-rise apartment windows, which didn't open, and see a ton of concrete. I was always used to lots of trees and grass around wherever I lived. Even in my apartment in North Dallas, I lived on the first floor and was on a beautiful golf course near the ladies' tee box. There were lots of trees and between me and the course a beautiful creek that sounded like a Colorado river after a big rain. I could open my windows and let the beautiful sounds of nature be there in that little place. I really loved it and had only lived there for four years. I told ML I wasn't ready to give that up. The upkeep of any apartment, I learned, was nil compared to owning a house. He was good with that, so he moved into the apartment, which was a 30-minute drive from his studio, where he spent a lot of time.

ML owned his own business, Noonday Pictures. It was a film studio that shot live-action food commercials, also called, "table top." The great thing about his job was that when he wasn't shooting commercials and was off, we could travel. We traveled a lot. He did warn me with, "Plan a trip, get a job." That did happen a few times. I would plan a trip and sure enough he would get a commercial job. More times than not we got to go on our planned trips. His job was fascinating to me. Watching the crew film the food commercials for restaurants I had seen on television for years. He had been doing Dairy Queen for most of his 30-year career. I got to watch Luby's, McDonald's, Taco Bell, Taco Bueno, Joe's Crab Shack and many more commercials be filmed at his studio. What I was fascinated with the most were the food stylists. They could make the food look so appetizing with all their trade secrets. When ML and I started dating and the stylists found out that I was a nurse, they were so excited. They asked me if there was any way I could get them some syringes and needles to use on the food shots. I told them, "Sure thing." Nurses have really big pockets to carry all our paraphernalia in while on duty. I stocked mine with some syringes and needles. In a couple of days, I went back to the studio while they were shooting a job and gave the needles and syringes to the stylists. I watched them as they went to work on the hero sandwich they were putting together for the "perfect shot!" They would take the syringe, fill it with a semi liquid sauce. They would squeeze the syringe and the needle would put the sauce between the layers of meat. The sauce would slowly ooze out of the layers of the sandwich, while ML would shoot it with his motion-control camera. It looked amazing to the clients, who loved the way ML and the stylists made their product look. ML told me that sometimes when shooting food they would actually make it look so good the client would go to him and tell him that the shot of their food looked way too good. They were afraid their customers would want to purchase what they saw on television, not what they would actually get. So basically he had to tone it down.

Those were the good days for him. There were also many days when the client was extremely picky. This made for some much longer shooting days than the normal 12-hour day. On occasion they would be much longer. I can remember one job he was doing where they were out very late. ML called me around 11 at night and said, "Having lots of problems, gotta go, gonna be late!" I went to bed knowing that ML would be really late. He dragged in around three in the morning and fell into bed. When we got up next day, I asked, "What in the heck happened last night that kept you guys shooting so late?" He said, "The client wanted the cheese melt to look a specific way and we were having the hardest time making it work. Finally, one of the guys came up with a contraption that would heat the cheese just the way the client wanted and we eventually got the shot she wanted." Rough days.

ML is loved by all my family. My parents especially warmed up to him. ML actually liked my parents and they knew he did. So I felt so grateful that this relationship was safe and comfortable. Those were the words I loved to use when I talk about ML and me. Comfortable and safe. We are just so comfortable together and are kind to each other. ML didn't have a large extended family. He has a daughter who is an attorney in Houston and a son who lives in Dallas and has a wife and a baby. The only other relative he had any contact with was his Aunt Helen, whom I met. She lived in San Antonio. Other than that, there was no one that we ever visited. When he met me, he started going to all our family reunions from my mom and my dad's sides of the family. He was loving this family connection thing that I had. This is something that if you have it you truly take it for granted, because there are so many people who have no idea who their relatives are, much less see them a couple of times a year. ML especially started getting close to my second cousin Cindy's husband, Tony. Cindy was more like a first cousin but who's counting! When my cousin Cindy met ML, she fell in love with him, and from then on called him "My Love" in lieu of ML! She's crazy fun! We have spent a lot of time with them on their ranch and ML hangs onto every word Tony says about ranch life and vice versa with Tony to ML. I am so grateful that our relationship could add so much to ML's lack of family with his interest in mine. Since then I have done a lot of research on Ancestry. com to find some of his "missing" relatives and have had a little success.

ML was also okay with some of my changed behaviors since all my counseling. Thank goodness he didn't know the old me. I'll give you an example. Playing golf with ML presented itself with some responses that most people find odd. When ML would hit a bad shot onto the green and I would drive the cart up, I never asked him if he wanted his putter because I learned the answer to that was, "If I can't shoot any better than that, I don't deserve to use a putter!" I would just walk to the green and watch him putt with his six iron or whatever was in his hand. When we would play with some of my girlfriends, they were puzzled with this and would yell at ML and ask, "ML, do you want me to get your putter?" He would respond, "No!" They would get it for him anyway and bring it to him. It never bothered him that I didn't coddle him. He is a very independent guy, which I learned early on and appreciated the fact that he didn't try to control me and I didn't try to control him. ML told me early on in our relationship that if there was ANYTHING I wanted to know I should not be shy or afraid to ask him. After all I had been through, I definitely ended up asking him some hard and invasive questions, and he always answered them and never hesitated to show me his cellphone or tell me who was calling him when his phone would ring. I was very insecure with the cellphone. As you might guess, this was a very pleasant change in my relationship dynamics.

ML came along too late and never really got to see the "best" of James. When things started going downhill with James, we would tell ML about him and how he had changed. We were all worried about where James would end up. In fact, we started dating in May 2005 and we were getting really close when the first episode happened to James in Nashville in December 2005. He went through most of the next five years with me and my kids in dealing with James. I am so grateful to have a loving and kind man to stand with me and give me lots of hugs in this sad time of my life. Whenever we would be with James, ML would be especially patient when I wasn't. I would be pleading, "Why did you do that?" And ML would just listen to James and not try to figure him out.

After we married in 2006, we continued to live in the apartment, but in the meantime my family of kids and grand-kids was growing. We still were not ready to buy a house, but we did go look at some lots and played some golf at this resort area around Lake Whitney called White Bluff. We ended up buying a small lot and that gave us golf rounds and discounts on the condos they had for us to stay in. It was the greatest getaway for us during those hard times with James. It was only an hour and forty-five minutes away from our apartment. We contemplated building a house on our lot but decided to just stay put and not make any big decisions at that time because of James.

ML and I were still going to Fellowship Dallas in 2009. James was in Fort Worth, struggling. ML and I were leaders of a small community group that met once a week at ML's studio. It was a sweet group of around seven of us from church. From the beginning of this group until we broke up, I always had James on the prayer list. After church one Sunday, we were visiting with some friends in the foyer area. Rob came up to visit and say hi. I thought he wanted to talk to me but instead he said, "I came to ask ML something." ML said, "What's up?" "I truly believe the Lord spoke to me and wants me to ask you to go to Sudan with us on a mission trip." ML was stunned. I knew he would say "no way" because he had always told me he never wanted to travel out of the country. He wouldn't go to Mexico and I was sure this meant he would not ever go to Africa, especially Sudan. At that time they were in the middle of a terrible power struggle with lots of people getting killed, raped or kidnapped. I just stood by to see his reaction. He actually pondered the question. I was really stunned when he told Rob, "Let me pray about it."

When we got home we started talking about it. I told him, "There is no way I want you to go to Sudan!" He told me, "Since the Lord has brought me back to Himself by forgiving me and helping me grow in my faith, I feel like this is something He wants me to reach out and do." What could I say to that? I still let him know that I wasn't totally on board. ML called Rob and said that he wanted to go.

So the preparations for him to go to Sudan began. The shots, the passport and packing. There was a group of other members from the church we didn't know who were going too. In all they had a group of five people going. They went in November and were gone around 12 days. Of course, I was praying daily for their safety and provision. The trip was successful. They all got back safe and sound. Thank you, Lord! ML fell in love with Sudan and the people. He described to me the living conditions they had and their joy! This was his first experience with any kind of evangelical experience and his first time to be in Africa. He told me he was going back. Well, by then I had sort of surrendered to his love of the Sudanese people.

CHAPTER 21

HEAVEN AND HELL ON EARTH

God is our refuge and strength, a very present
help in time of trouble. Therefore, we will not fear,
though the earth should change.

PSALM 46:1-2

Thou art my hiding place; Thou dost preserve
me from trouble; Thou dost surround me
with songs of deliverance.

PSALM 32:7

Life was moving forward with Johnny and Christy both married. I had three grandkids and Katie, Johnny's wife, was pregnant. She was due in October of 2010. ML and I were still going to White Bluff and playing golf on some weekends. ML had told me that if I wanted to retire from nursing he didn't see why I didn't. I had spent the last two years not working very much because I took care of my dad who had quadruple bypass surgery at the end of 2007. In 2008, my mom had both knees replaced at the same time. That was a huge recovery so I spent a lot of time in Breckenridge. I agreed with ML and stopped working as a nurse, because like I would say, "I want to spend my time now with my little grandkids and play some golf." This is exactly what I was doing.

James was still tossing about and having a hard time. On holidays, he would say he was coming but he would end up a no-show. In 2009, the last Christmas he would see, he went with ML and me to Breckenridge for a big family Christmas with all the cousins, aunts and uncles present. Before we started out for Breckenridge, after picking James up in Fort Worth, it started to snow heavily. We thought we might have to turn around because of the roads. I called my dad and asked what he thought and he said the roads were snowy but not icy. Off we headed to Breckenridge and ended up arriving safe and sound for a beautiful snowy Christmas.

James was so happy to be with his cousins and grandparents. Just to be in his favorite place in the world, Breckenridge, Texas. We had a great time with everyone. Lots of laughs, lots of playing in the snow for all. Like when they were all 10 years old and were innocent kids with not a care in the world. But you could feel the heaviness around James that none of his cousins could feel, except Wesley and Ashley, who knew about all that had happened to him in Nashville. Once this respite was over, we took him back to Fort Worth to move on into the New Year – 2010.

He started dating a new girl named Nena. I didn't get to meet her until the spring of 2010 at Pete's. James didn't really seem crazy about her like he was about Crystal. He was getting a lot of tickets for no license, no insurance and speeding. Almost every time I went to Fort Worth it was a "rescue mission." He would have banking problems and then off to Bank America we would go, insurance problems with his car, off to Fred Loya, car trouble, mechanic, on and on. I found out later from my son-in-law that James was paying his tickets off by staying in the jail cell to work them off. I also found out that my dad was giving my son-in-law, Greg, money to help James out. I kept seeing that there was a disconnect in James' brain that created a disconnect from inner and outer reality. He could not figure out his role as a responsible adult or how to cope in an unimagined world. There was no meaning to him for the words *common sense* – useful notions, shared symbols and socially acceptable ways of doing the most common of things. This was a very hard thing for a mother to see and not have any idea what it was, where it came from and mostly how to fix it! I would go see him most of the times he would call. He wouldn't call me in difficult situations, so I figured between him and his buddies they would work things out.

ML and I continued to go to White Bluff and loved it more and more. In late winter 2009, we were staying in the condo for a snowy weekend. We saw the beautiful snow falling on Lake Whitney and saw the deer leaping through it. So peaceful. We started talking and decided we wanted to get a house there after all. I called the lady whose name was on all the for-sale houses in White Bluff. We told her we wanted to look at what was available and not too big. She showed us several nice houses but mostly they just had a large master, large great room and maybe a small study and small guest room. I started thinking about our family and how much I knew it would grow. I asked her to show us something larger. She took us to see a beautiful house that we both fell in love with. It was big and on one of the two golf courses. It was a beautiful treed lot with great views all around and no other houses next to it. We would talk about it and all the what-ifs. We knew this place would be perfect for our family to have a place to come for family gatherings. I likened it to my kids having Breckenridge when they were little. A place to escape from the city, enjoy nature, swim in the four pools on the property, play tennis on the courts, play lots of golf and fish in the lake on the golf course behind the house. It was ideal for what we wanted. I spoke to the realtor and gave her an unusually low price for the house, because like I told her, "We don't have to buy a house, but if this deal works we are in." After talking to the seller's realtor, the seller came back with the response, "According to our divorce decree we cannot go below this price." So we got that beautiful home for $64 a square foot in December of 2009. By February we closed and it was ours. It had three stories, and in the next five months we remodeled the main middle floor and the other floors were perfect. In the meantime, James had gotten the job at Pete's Dueling Piano Bar and was working several nights a week. His boss wanted him to work more. James was tiring of the hours and the drinking. I think he was hearing a lot of voices during this time but not telling anyone or drugging them over with alcohol or marijuana.

On all my drives back and forth to White Bluff, I would have long prayer sessions for James. Lots of crying and interceding on his behalf. I was also listening to lots of CDs in my car about believing, faith and prayer. One weekend, we invited Mom and Dad to White Bluff and we spent an entire afternoon watching a great DVD on prayer by Jim Cymbala. After listening to the hearttouching DVD, we all cried, got on our knees and started praying for James. Prayers for God's intercession to save James from himself and heal whatever was wrong with his brain. We had peace after we were done.

It was like a crescendo, the way the events started moving. James wanted us to see him perform at Pete's. We were all so excited to see him perform, we invited a couple of friends who lived in Fort Worth. Janice and Josh came. It was here that I met Nena, but it was weird because Crystal happened to be there too, and I was so glad to see her. I really don't remember why she was there that night but she was. Of course we were the earlier, less rowdy crowd at Pete's that night, but we took up a lot of seats that might otherwise be empty if we all hadn't shown up. Before the show started, James came out to say hi to all of us and give us lots of hugs and photos! He looked great and happy. I was proud of him. The place opened at seven so we were there to get seats up close. The show started at eight.

Showtime! Out comes James and he sits himself down on the piano bench and starts banging on the pearly whites. I was amazed as we all were! He had been transformed. I knew he could play, but this was way out of the park. All the greats at a piano bar he had mastered, and as the show got going the audience was participating. The fun was happening. The crowd singing along with "Sweet Caroline." Girls called up to sit on the piano with James and his partner singing to them. "Friends in Low Places," "Chantilly Lace" and "I Love Rock and Roll," just to name a few.

They had a really great show and it went over without a hitch. The tip jars were filling up and it was still early. I knew that these guys really made their money after 10 till close at two in the morning.

Of course, we were out of there before those hours. We talked about it all the way back to Dallas.

We left and didn't even really think about what James was going through during these late-night shows. He had to deal with really drunk customers, girls flirting with the piano guys and the customers who kept buying them shots because the bar has to make a lot of money. It is not good, especially for someone like James who doesn't live in reality or can't separate reality from this. If I hadn't been so hopeful for him after being there and realized what this was doing to him, I would probably have talked to him about all of it. I was just happy to see him happy, doing something with his talent and making some money. He made a lot of money in the small span of time he worked there. He would go on spending sprees and buy instruments at Guitar Center then return them. Some of his paychecks he never actually cashed. I found some of them in papers he had among his effects after he died. The reality of money was something his brain could not get hold of.

About two months after we saw him is when I got the call from Greg in Fort Worth that James was on the billboard naked. This was the climax of the crescendo that was happening in 2010. After the police finally got James to slide down the billboard because of the extreme change in weather, they took him to the JPS psych ward to be admitted. They never made a formal arrest. It was a mental issue and he was never charged with anything during that whole time.

The world stood still as we all left Fort Worth to go home. Numb and not knowing what tomorrow would bring. I did know that the Lord would hold our hand and be with us during this dark time. He says in Hebrews 13:5, "I will never leave you or forsake you." I knew that, deep down in my spirit and my soul. I have lived it and seen what He has done in my life and where He has led. So this time He was still the same God the Father that I have always had near me and all of my family during tough times. I called the hospital where James was taken and spoke to the nurse. She said I could come and see him in a day or two. We waited and prayed. Lisa wanted to go with me to see James. He ended up staying there for about 10 days. I got the call to go see him. Lisa and I drove to Fort Worth and went into the psych ward at John Peter Smith hospital. We got to sit alone with him in a room with the door open. When he saw us, he was all over us hugging and begging us to get him out. We talked about what had happened. He was not repentant and actually laughed when Lisa asked him if he remembered what had happened to him, being on the billboard naked for six hours. He never told us that he heard voices like he had told Tanson and Kolby before he jumped off the balcony to run to the billboard. He was on medication to keep him calm, but he still was lucid enough to talk with us. He was extremely sunburned from being on the billboard for such an extended time.

During this time, all the cousins and buddies were very anxious about his possible drug use. Some thought he had been high on quaaludes, mushrooms or lots of marijuana. The drug tests they did on him were clear of any alcohol or drugs other than marijuana. He admitted to the nurses that he was a daily marijuana user. While he was at JPS, he would tell the nurses that voices were talking to him through the television in the community room. Tanson would call him on the floor phone and play him some of his favorite songs. This really seemed to calm James down. Lisa would call him and all he wanted to know from her was when he was getting out and going back to work at Pete's. She would tell him he wasn't going to get out for a while because he really needed a lot of help. When she would talk to him like that, he would hang up. In the meantime, I got power of attorney over his health and could make decisions as to where he would be treated and hospitalized. Finally, the director and James' doctor called a meeting for Lisa and me. In the meantime, I was having no luck with anyone taking James for treatment because they didn't make their patients stay. They could just walk out, and we knew that if we put James in one of these places he would bolt. James had been in the JPS psych ward for about 10 days when we had the meeting with the director and doctor. They started talking about James' condition and we all agreed that he needed in-patient care, because he was still very delusional about his illness and reality. They told us that they could send James to one of the State hospitals and he would be in a locked-down unit. They suggested 30-45 days. I started crying and said, "I feel so guilty about all of this for James!" The director looked at me and said emphatically, "I RELEASE you from feeling guilty. You did not do this to him. This is not your fault." They told us that he would leave for Wichita Falls State Hospital in a couple of days. They told us we could go visit him a couple of days a week. It was a two-hour drive. We were relieved that he would be under their watch for a while.

We didn't have to worry about his care. We truly thought they might help him during this time of confinement. Toward the end of the meeting with them, Lisa and I were weeping. Then the doctor reached across the table and said, "I hate to tell you, but these things don't usually end well." I could see the look of sorrow in her face, as she probably did this many times when having to talk to other families about their mentally ill family members.

James arrived at Wichita Falls State Hospital on May 14th, about 11 days after the billboard incident, and we really couldn't see much progress.

I would make the two-hour drive to see him twice a week. I would bring him a Subway sandwich and talk to him for about an hour. Sometimes we would go outside and sit on the patio, looking around and seeing the big fences. This hospital sat on some very serene country property just south of Wichita Falls. He always seemed so calm, but not content. I couldn't tell if it was the meds he was on or him. I would watch the people around him and the friends he told me he was making. James seemed so much more sane than the people who were moping around, shuffling and mumbling under their breath. But as I would watch these young men, I would always think to myself, they belong to some mom or dad somewhere. When we would visit, he was lucid, sweet and calm. But there was the undertone of him wanting to get out and play with his band. In spite of his appearance of sanity, he still had hope for his future and fantasies. I could just not see any of it happening, considering the recent events and his current circumstances. During his time at Wichita Falls, we were praying and believing the Lord would find us the right place to take him after his time there was over. One of Lisa's best friends was looking for a place for him to go after he got out.

They had told us that they could only keep him for four weeks. He ended up staying there for six weeks. With the help of some great family friends of Lisa, we had a list of halfway houses that we thought would be good for him, but the next hurdle was to get them to be willing to take him with his history. Lisa was glued to my hip all during this process. Her best friend, Shannon, had found us a home that she thought would be perfect for James. Shannon had known James since he was four years old. I told her we would try and get an interview with them. The Gaston House was a home for young men who could not get their life together for one reason or another. Mostly their underlying problems were addiction related and just a lack of ability to grow up. Lisa and I were praying that Chico and his staff would take James in.

Lisa at this point was pressing me on how I knew we were making the right decisions about James. I came right out and honestly told her that I wasn't absolutely sure that what we were doing was what the Lord wanted, but one thing I did know was that He was in charge of me, and I knew that when my heart and mind were inclined to do something that was my "YES, move forward." So I told her that in situations like this you just take it one step at a time and don't look back. It is a slippery slope, but the only choice you have as a believer is to believe that when you are totally walking by faith that in the process the decisions you make are made by faith and according to what He wants you to do. My response to her seemed to help her. It helped me to verbalize it.

Chico called me from Gaston House and told me the staff had made their decision about James and they wanted us to come and talk to them. ML, Lisa and I arrived at Gaston House. We prayed with tears out in the front yard that this would end up okay. We walked into the Gaston House living room and the whole staff was there to talk to us. As we got settled and met everyone, Chico led the discussion. He started where I was hoping. The first words out of his mouth were, "We've checked out all of James' records and have decided that we think that we are going to be able to take him and hopefully help him." Lisa, ML and I started crying and hugging each other and proceeded to hug all the staff in the room in gratitude of their generosity for letting him be a part of the Gaston House recovery program. The meeting became just routine about how he was going to be processed and what would be required of him and us while he was a client of theirs. This meeting occurred about five days before James was released from the Wichita Falls hospital. The next day, I went to Wichita Falls and told James that he was going to the Gaston House when the hospital released him. He was not happy. He wanted to get out and go live with his band buddies in Denton. You could tell that in his imagination he had endured all this and was going to be free now to live wherever he wanted, but this was not exactly in the true picture. So on July 2, 2010, ML and I picked James up from the hospital in Wichita Falls. You could see the relief when we left the campus and hit Highway 287 heading east to Dallas. Once we got near Denton, he started to panic and pleaded with us to drop him off in Denton at David's house, one of his band buddies. He kept telling us, "I will be fine. Please, Mom!" He was so persistent. He was begging us, it was so sad. He truly believed that this was his salvation. To be part of David's band in Denton and forget about all the events that had preceded this. I was seeing my son lose all control of his life. Now he would be dependent on people who would help him, hopefully. We finally got to the Gaston House and the staff member that was there was someone I was not familiar with. He said that Chico and the other clients and counselors were in Austin for the 4th of July weekend but James would be okay until they got home in a few days. I was a little hesitant because Chico was not there to meet him, but I believed they were okay with this.

The next morning I got a call from Gaston House that James was gone and they didn't know where he was. I figured that when James knew that the "powers that be" were not there, it was a perfect time for him to hitch a ride to Fort Worth to see his buddies. Somehow he got a ride to Fort Worth on the Trinity Railway Express. His buddies and his girlfriend met him and let him stay a few days. After being with his buddies on the night of the 4th of July, the next day they told him that they did not want him to be with them, that he was sick and needed help. He needed to go back to the Gaston House. This was the last night he spent with them. The next morning, he went back to the Gaston House. When he arrived, Chico and the guys had just gotten back from Austin and greeted James. Chico called me and told me that James had left but came back. I was so hoping that he wouldn't kick James out of the program.

James started to get connected to the program and started to comply with their rules and help. David was his counselor and told me he loved James and really felt like they could help him. My hopes were high. I was feeling confident that this place and people were going to be good for him. James was still begging me to get him out and let him go to Denton to play with his band. That was so hard. My counselor, Rob, told me that I should stay strong and keep him at the Gaston House and tell James that he needed to stay where he was. One day at a time, James was at the Gaston House, making friends with the other guys there, who were mostly recovering drug or alcohol addicts. The guys loved James. He entertained them, sang for them and told them jokes.

Then the time came when he had to get a job and earn some money, part of the program. They got him a job at the Starbucks just up the road on Gaston Avenue. He could walk. He would tell me that he loved the people he worked with, but he neglected to tell me how hard it was for him to do the cash transactions and make change. Later at James' funeral, the kids from Starbucks told me that they loved James and did all they could to help him make change in awkward ways so as not to embarrass him. Bless his heart, I never knew how much he missed or faked in school to make him unable later on to operate in the basics of business. I know he knew how inadequate he was when he got this job. They never fired him. He had this job until he died, and at his funeral all his Starbuck crew were there in force in their uniforms to pay tribute to James.

James continued to stay and work at the Gaston House. He never ran away again. Between ML and me, Lisa and Johnny, we would take him to lunch and talk to him. Whenever any of us saw him, all he wanted to talk about was us getting him out and taking him to Denton. This got really old for all of us.

He was still talking on the phone to his girlfriend, Nena. He was so afraid she was going to break up with him since he was in Dallas getting mental health treatment and she was in Fort Worth. I think it was about that time that he started planning on sneaking out and going back to Fort Worth to try and win her back. Another delusion. The Gaston House had set him up with a psychologist, who prescribed Celexa. I'm not sure if he ever took it. He was not on any antipsychotics like he had been in the hospital.

All during the next few months, he would go to work at Starbucks, go to AA meetings, have support meetings at the Gaston House and do chores with guys around the house. He would call Lisa and she would pick him up to go eat Mexican food. ML and I would take him out to eat when he was available, but the pleading and begging got so bad that my counselor, Rob, told us to not go see him for a while.

The crescendo was starting toward the end.

CHAPTER 22

BEGINNING OF THE END

Thou, O Lord, wilt not withhold Thy
compassion from me; Thy loving kindness and
Thy truth will continually preserve me; for evils beyond
number have surrounded me; my iniquities have overtaken
me, so that I am not able to see; they are more numerous
that the hairs of my head; my heart has failed me.

PSALM 40:11-12

On September 23, James asked Nena to come pick him up at the Gaston House. She helped him to do a video call with some doctor from India who faxed him Risperdal, an antipsychotic drug. He was already in the care of a psychologist with the Gaston House and on Celexa. After they did this, she dropped him off and told him she was breaking up with him.

On Saturday, September 25, ML and I were on an evening with ML's son's new love and about to meet her parents. It was getting late in the evening and we were at his girlfriend's parents' house. My phone rang and I took the call outside of their home. It was Johnny and Katie. At this point, Katie was nine months pregnant and could deliver at any moment. Johnny sounded desperate. He was telling me that James was calling them and wanting them to come pick him up and get him out of Gaston House. They did pick him up and took him out to dinner. They, tearfully, took him back to Gaston House. Johnny called me pleading, "Mom, James is desperate! Why don't you get him out? If you do, he can come live with us!" I asked Johnny, "Do you really want James with you and Katie in the condition he's in and Katie about ready to have her first child? You have no idea what he may do." He knew that wouldn't work. They never went back to see James. After that, I was a basket case. I called David a day later and he let me know that James was doing fine.

On Tuesday, September 28, David took James to Dr. Clemens, his psychologist, and told him the whole story. The doctor told James not to go to another doctor but to keep seeing him. They added Abilify to his regimen. On that day, home from the doctor's office, David said he felt a strong opportunity to ask James about his relationship with Jesus. James told him that Jesus was in his heart and he was sure that he was a child of the Father. David felt more hopeful for James. On Wednesday, September 29, James took a week off of work from Starbucks. I believe that James had a plan to leave Gaston House and go to Nena's in Fort Worth, but she rebuffed him and said not to come.

On Thursday, September 30, James and David did some cleaning at Gaston House. This day was James' 24th birthday. My brother, Russ, picked him up to have some fun. David told James, "Get out of your head and have some fun with your Uncle Russ." The afternoon they had was full of fun with Russ and his office manager, Tracey, who loved James. They had a great birthday cake, but in the end they had to take him back to Gaston House. It was that night as the fun ended that James shared with David that Nena broke up with him. I spoke with him on the phone on our way to Breckenridge to see my parents. He sounded happy and upbeat. Never said anything about Nena breaking up with him.

After Russ dropped James back off at Gaston House, he was playing the piano for the guys and singing to entertain them all. David told me that that night was the one night where James seemed to be hitting it off at the Gaston House. After most of the guys went to bed, James was still up playing the piano.

When the time to tone it down came, James went into the kitchen. He got a new steak knife out of the drawer and went to the gym on the upstairs room on top of the outdoor garage. He took his Bible and opened it to Nehemiah. What occurred after this is between him and his Maker. But I truly believe that under the influence of the Destroyer, Satan, he was told to take the knife he had brought with him and pierce himself four times. That is what happened. James realized what he had done and he knew that he needed help, as usual, to get him out of this trauma. I believe that once he came to himself, he ran down the stairs then ran up the stairs to his room in the big house. He grabbed his roommate and told him, "Hey man, I've done something really stupid! Take me to the hospital and they will know what to do!" His blessed roommate and some of the other guys nearby wrapped his chest in towels. They realized that he had stabbed himself in four places in his left chest. There was not a lot of external bleeding, but unbeknownst to them or James, the heart was perforated and a tragedy was occurring before they ever knew. Like the *Titanic*, the awful tragedy was happening deep under water. Once they got him to Baylor, which was very close to the Gaston House, the hospital was ready for him and James was still alert and told the guys, "Wait for me, I'll be back." Which was in contrast to what he told the surgeon before he went under. He told the attending surgeon, "Don't even bother, you are dealing with a dead man." James could feel his life ebbing away. I choose to believe that it was during this time that he was seeing his future in the kingdom of Heaven. It took only an hour and it was over.

They couldn't save him and placed the call to me. They called my cellphone.

That night as I was going to bed at my parents' house, I put my phone next to my bed, which I never do there. Around three in the morning, my phone rang and I didn't recognize the number. I answered anyway. The lady said she was calling from Baylor Hospital in Dallas and that my son, James Apple, was in their care. She said I needed to get there as soon as possible. I told her that I was three hours away but that I would call James' sister to come since she only lived 30 minutes from Baylor. I inquired what had happened and she said that since he was no longer a minor she could not share anything about him to me … HIPAA laws. I was irate. I called Lisa and told her to go to Baylor and check on James then call me with any information she got. After I hung up, I had a very angry tirade at the foot of the bed while my husband, who was awake by now, just watched. He kept asking me what was going on. I was so upset because it wasn't the first time I'd gotten "the call" about James. I was just plain unadulterated angry at James. In about an hour, I got a call from a sobbing daughter and the only thing she said to me was, "Mom, James didn't make it. He's gone!" I was catastrophically devastated and stunned. How can this happen?! She put the surgeon on the line and he said they did everything they could to save his life. He had stabbed himself in the left ventricle of his heart and three other places. There was so much internal bleeding that they couldn't contain it or fix it. In the past, whenever James got himself in some trouble they were always able to fix him. I was shocked and didn't understand, since I had just talked to him eight hours ago. But not this day. There was nothing they could do, only Jesus could fix him … he would die on the operating table and lose his life.

I learned later from his counselor, David, that James had seemed to be doing well except that he was upset because his girlfriend, Nena, broke up with him and that upset him a lot. I found out from his buddies that he was planning on leaving Dallas and going back to Fort Worth, but when Nina told him that she wanted out he had no option but to stay in Dallas. I really think this was the last straw for James. He couldn't see anything working out, and I truly believed he lost hope for himself. He had lost all power and control over his choices. So he believed he was better off just ending it all. We started out from Breckenridge to Dallas after Lisa's call. I felt so bad that she had to go through all that alone. But come to find out, all the Gaston House crew were there in the ICU waiting area with her as she had to identify James' body. Greg, Johnny and Katie were there also. The ICU social worker could tell that this crowd of mourners was only getting larger, so she moved everyone into a larger private room. When ML and I finally got to the parking lot at Baylor Hospital, I could not get out of the truck. It was a surreal experience. I kept telling ML, "No, no, no! If I get out then I am admitting that this has really happened! And James is gone!" I didn't want to do that. Finally, he pried me out of the passenger seat and got me into the elevator to take us up to the ICU floor where James was. As soon as we walked into the room where everyone was, I fell apart. Our friends, Janice and Josh, Ed and Susan, were there along with about 25 guys from Gaston House and my own children. I sat in Johnny's lap and cried my eyes out. It was the hardest thing I have ever been through in my life.

The ICU nurse came out when she found out we were there. "Do you want to go see James?" Of course I did, but this was a real turnaround from my being an ICU nurse myself, and having to ask the same question to my deceased patients' family members. I grabbed Lisa and took her with me to see him. He had large bandages all over his chest, but other than that he looked so peaceful and serene. He was so beautiful and his hair looked great. His skin, his hair, his body looked perfect except for the bandages taped to his chest. I said to him, "Wake up, James, wake up! This can't be happening!" Lisa left me alone with him. After a while in the peace of the moment, I was alone with my youngest son's dead body. I knew that he was not there. I could actually feel him looking down at me and saying, "Mom, I'm okay now." I gave him a big hug and told him, "Goodbye, sweetheart, give everyone else up there a big hug! And by the way, have a lot of fun! Up there, you can live like you want to and there are not as many rules to follow as there are down here."

It was only a week later that I got a copy of the autopsy report. While reading it, I was amazed that every organ in his body was perfect. The only flaw was the self-inflicted fatal flaws in his heart.

CHAPTER 23

SAYING GOODBYE

Jesus said unto her, I am the Resurrection and the Life;
he who believes in Me shall live even if he dies, and
everyone who lives and believes in Me shall never die.

JOHN 11:25

Why do you seek the living One among the dead?
He is not here, but He has risen.

LUKE 24:5-6

The ICU waiting room was full of emotion, pain and bewilderment. It was like walking through a nightmare. You could feel the love that everyone had for James. I realized that we needed to let a lot of people know. Between all my kids we called everyone who knew and loved James. My oldest daughter, Christy, wasn't at the hospital because she had to stay home with her three babies. I really don't think she could have emotionally handled this trauma of losing her baby brother. Christy went into survival mode and started making funeral plans. She called the funeral planner at our church, our friend Carol. Carol was also part of the South Sudan mission trip that ML went on the year before. James passed away around two in the morning of October 1, 2010, three hours into his 24th year of life. Looking back at James' beginning and end … he was born in Breckenridge and I learned of his death when I was in Breckenridge. Not a coincidence.

By the time our family left Baylor, we knew who we wanted to do the funeral and the date. It was set up for October 4 at 11 AM at Fellowship Bible Church Dallas and I wanted Rob to do the service. We called him while we were at Baylor and he met us later to figure out the service. He told us he really wanted to do the service. I was so relieved. Lisa was planning everything else, music and speakers. I told her I wanted to also say something. After we left Baylor, I told all our family to meet us at Prestonwood Country Club where we could talk and share. ML and I still had our small apartment and we needed a place with more room. The club was like our big living room. When we got there, of course there were lots of tears. Fortunately for us, we were the only people in the 19th Hole. I had also become a good friend with the food and beverage manager, Diane. I shared with her what was going on. She gave me a big hug and cried. She was very kind and sweet. She took good care of us. It was here that the funeral was planned. My sister also came to this meeting. Together we all made it through with the planning and the pain. On Sunday, I went to the funeral home with Lisa and Christy to plan the viewing and the funeral. I also told the funeral director that James was going to be buried in Throckmorton, Texas in my grandparents' plot. He would have to be transported there after the funeral and we would have the interment at the Throckmorton Cemetery. While we were ending up at the funeral home with the charges, etc., the funeral director asked me how I wanted to pay for this. I was dumbfounded and handed him my American Airlines Citibank card. It was quite a large tab. Christy and Lisa were sitting there with me. All I could say was, "I guess I might as well get some miles out of this!" Then I laughed. I had cried so hard for the last three days, it was a little bit of relief.

Mom and Dad got to Dallas on Monday to go to the viewing. Seeing them became a total tear fest. I was so glad they were there.

The viewing was on Monday night. There was quite the crowd of friends and relatives. I can't really remember much of what happened, just a mirage of people coming up and loving on me and telling me how sorry they were. James' dad, John Apple, was there. He hugged me and was sobbing uncontrollably. Next came husband number three, Duyane, who hugged me and was crying, telling me how sorry he was. We had put an obituary in the Dallas, Fort Worth and Breckenridge papers. So the word got out. I did go in and see James in the casket. He didn't look as good to me as he did in the hospital. I could only go in there once. He had more color and was softer looking in the hospital. By that time I really knew where he was and how vibrant he was in his new location. There were a lot of young people, though, who were in the viewing room crying over his casket. It was so sad. I looked across the room and I saw my sweet friend Ina, a secretary from Arlington ICU, walking in with her husband, John. I grabbed her and we both cried our eyes out!

When we got home that night, I sobbed like my guts were falling out. I cannot describe that gut-wrenching grief of losing a child. I could just be sitting on the couch and a wave of pain would sweep over me, gut-punch me and the deep moaning would start all over again. Loud and deep are the only words I can use to describe it. Pain comes to all of us at one time or another. Our expressions of this pain differ from one person to another. This pain with James' death is something I can't describe. If I could have worn sackcloth and ashes, I would have. Going through all this, I never got mad at God. I knew that He loved James way more than I ever could. I did have questions. Why didn't he get any better? What's the purpose of him being gone? I knew one day I would have the answers. This is the hope we believers have.

I eventually realized that James was not made to function in the world like my other three kids could. I truly believe the Lord looked down and saw all the pain and said, "Enough. You are coming home to Me." All your hopes and dreams for them, your heart entwined with theirs, and most of all the knowing that they were yours for a time on this earth. Then suddenly that is over. This is more than a human can endure. But, as in Daniel 2:28, "There is a God in heaven," and He is the one Who sustains us in our grief and gives us hope. He was really there for me. I was and am so grateful to be able to walk through all this pain in His love and in the knowledge that James is at peace.

I wanted to share at the funeral. Psalm 40 had been my scripture for James since 2005 with the psych incident in Nashville. It had been the bedrock of my hope for him.

This was the basis of my talk. The funeral was on Tuesday at Fellowship Bible Church in Dallas.

We got there early and, fortunately for ML, getting me out of the car was a much easier task than the past Saturday had been. I was resolute to the fact that James was redeemed and set free from his mental torture. As we walked in the north entrance, we saw James' old beat-up pickup that had been to hell and back. It was my dad's old pickup. This pickup was iconic "James" amongst his buddies. I know for a fact that many wild adventures had occurred in and on that pickup during James' 16th through 18th years. I never could figure out why the cab and trailer were not lined up correctly until one of his friends told me that James used the truck to pull off "Evel Knievel" tricks, jumping over large objects. There was also a bagpipe player outside playing "Amazing Grace." I found out later that this touch was added by my brother, James' Uncle Russ.

Carol, the funeral planner, had been gathering all our family members into the center downstairs from the chapel where the funeral was to take place. There were a lot of people there who were from both Mom and Dad's sides of the family. There were first, second and third cousins, uncles, aunts, great-uncles and great-aunts. You could see the disbelief in their eyes that James had died. A lot of these relatives knew James well and loved to be around him. They had no idea of the pain from the past five years. At all reunions from a young age, James had entertained those folks, loved and was friendly to the very oldest. He always had a kiss and a hug for everyone. You could tell the relatives that knew him since the beginning. They called him "Jamie." So many people were touched by James in his childhood years, because he loved people and wanted them all to feel good. He paid attention to everyone, young and old. Plus, there were friends who were like family that I wanted nearby. As we were all waiting in this room, which was getting very crowded, Carol came to me and said, "Kay, this is very strange, but we are going to have to make some changes." "Why, what is the matter?" I asked. She said that the chapel was overflowing and they were going to have to change the funeral from the chapel to the sanctuary. I said, "Sure, whatever you have to do." She said that it probably would delay the funeral for 45 minutes while they moved James' casket and set up all the audio/video for the sanctuary. I thought to myself, "This is so James." He always loved a great party and this was his going-away party, so of course it will be a "smash hit!"

As the family was gathered in this room away from the rest of the crowd, some stories were shared about James that were sweet reminders of how he touched relatives in ways that I never knew about.

While we were all in this room surrounded by glass, I could see people going up the escalator to the sanctuary. I happened to look out when all my golf buddies from Prestonwood Country Club passed by the window to go upstairs. They blew me kisses, grabbing their hearts. I kept crying. People loving on people. God is so good!

Finally, Carol came to me and said they were all set up and we could make the entrance in to the sanctuary. She also said, "Kay, this is amazing! You will not believe how many people are in the sanctuary to say goodbye to James, and especially young kids. He must have been an amazing kid!" I just kept thinking to myself that only James could have a funeral where there were so many people there to say goodbye that they had to change the venue before it even started. Off we went into the sanctuary. When we were walking in, I could see how many people, especially young people James' age, were there. I was overwhelmed.

As the family proceeded to be seated, the last ones to sit in front of James' casket were ML and me, my kids, and my mom and dad. On the row behind us were James' dad and his wife.

The music director of the church sang "It Is Well" to start us out – my request because it was well with my soul!

Christy read some scriptures with her brother Johnny standing next to her. Then I spoke with ML standing next to me. My scripture was Psalm 40, which had been my bedrock since December 2005 in Nashville. I spoke of James' broken heart and how he really was not made for this world. He really could not function and Jesus said to him, "Okay, James, it is over, you are coming home to ME!"

James' best friend, Tanson, spoke with deep, heartfelt, brotherly love and told some funny stories about James. One of the stories he told was when they were in high school and James told Tanson to get his video cam and follow him to the Mansfield Target store. James had on a red knit shirt and some khaki pants but was missing the Target name tag. He told Tanson to video him as he pretended to be a salesperson in the video area. Tanson dutifully obeyed and was standing by. A woman walked up to James as he was leaning down looking at the video games. Tanson's camera started. The lady asked, "Do you work here?" James said, "Oh, yes, ma'am. What may I help you with?" Cool as a cucumber, he pointed to a few games in the locked cabinet. He dutifully described each one of them. He gave her advice on which games he thought her son would love. To James' surprise, the lady said, "I want those games, please. Can you get them out and I will buy them." James responded, "Yes, ma'am, sure, but I really don't have the authority to unlock the cabinet. Let me go get someone with more authority than me who can help you." Off he and Tanson trotted to leave Target. Typical James story.

His cousin, Wesley, spoke next. He saw firsthand James' delusions in Nashville and spoke of his love and admiration for James. He totally admired the talent James had been given and was so sad that it never reached fruition on this earth. Wes never had a brother, but he always considered James as close or closer than one. They had a lot in common with their music talents. He also had a few funny stories to tell. One story was about my brother Russ and James. He said that James and Russ had gone to Walmart. James just wanted to wait in the car so Russ went in without him. After a while James got bored and started looking around the truck. He saw a lot of rolls of toilet paper in the back seat. He started to wind himself up with the paper. He proceeded to walk in to Walmart completely covered with toilet paper. He was walking like a zombie with his arms stretched out in front of him, up and down the aisles, calling out Russ' name. Russ eventually found him and hauled him out of the store.

Wes also shared about the demons that tormented James. At first it was "just James," but after what he saw James do in his apartment in Nashville, he knew there was much more to this than any of our family knew. By the time Wes finished, there was not a dry eye in the place. I guarantee you that with all the young people there, each one had a story about James. Rob Sherman did the sermon, and as he spoke there was not a dry eye either. He had a picture of James put on the big screen. James was playing a grand piano, probably at Russell's studio. His head was tilted, giving him a very peaceful and relaxing demeanor. His upper body, shoulders and legs looked totally at ease. Rob said, "Look how relaxed James is in this picture. This is where James knew who he was. He knew playing the piano was where he could really be himself. This is why playing the piano is the only thing that brought him peace and some sense of self. Everything outside of this was his non-reality." He also spoke of addictions and how we all struggled to live a full life on this earth. His message touched so many of the people present.

Lisa was last to speak. She had some sweet words and spoke of the memories of her and James' symbiotic relationship. They were truly a lot alike. She played a song she had written about James right after the billboard incident. She titled it "Jamie," which is what we all called him until he was in kindergarten when I went with him to meet his teacher. She leaned down to him and asked him, "Well, Jamie, what do you want me to call you in class?" He emphatically looked at her and then to me and said, "James!" It was James from then on, except with his grandparents and relatives who knew him from the time he was little. That song was the perfect ending to a beautiful send-off for a beautiful young man who is deeply loved and sorely missed.

After the funeral, we went out into the foyer to greet our friends and family. Everyone was so sweet and loving. I looked up and in the distance I saw this redhead coming toward me. I realized who it was. It was Patti, my friend from high school, Young Life and TCU. I raced toward her. We hugged big time. I knew she lived in Kansas and I had lost contact with her, so I didn't have her phone number. I couldn't believe she was there. She told me that she had a friend from Kansas who was now living in Dallas. She said the friend had kids who told her about James' death and told her what had happened. Patti did some research and realized that I was James' mother. She got on a plane and showed up immediately. We spent the rest of the day together. I told her all that had happened to James. It was a terrible way to reconnect, but we did and have had the opportunity to stay connected. God works in mysterious ways! I spent the next day driving to Throckmorton with my dear friend Dena riding with me to the interment. She was out of town for the funeral but she wanted to go with me to Throckmorton. ML drove to Throckmorton with Rob, who spoke at the graveside service and was speaking at the interment. It was comforting for me to see James placed so closely to my granddad and grandma and eventually my dad, mom, me and ML. This is where I decided I wanted to be buried, next to James and my family and in a place I loved. Many of James' close friends were at the graveside service. It was very special. After the service, most of us drove back to Breckenridge. We spent the afternoon at Mom and Dad's ranch eating some great food brought in by friends and family and having a wonderful time sharing.

CHAPTER 24

THE AFTERMATH

Who shall separate us from the love of Christ? Shall tribulation, or distress, or persecution, or famine, or nakedness, or peril, or sword? But in all these things we overwhelmingly conquer through Him who loved us. For I am convinced that neither death, nor life, nor angels, nor principalities, nor things present, nor things to come, nor powers, nor height, nor depth, nor any other created thing, shall be able to separate us from the love of God, which is in Christ Jesus our Lord.
ROMANS 8:37-39

The end was upon us. No more get-togethers. It was back to living in the real world, where James could not function, and remembering him in the best ways we could. There were a lot of Facebook posts made on a group site someone set up for him called RIP James Apple! I loved reading these posts. I laughed and I cried. It was time to go back to living. Wherever I went after the funeral … to the nail salon, the hair salon and golf outings … I was crying and sharing. A very sad time, but it was healing for me to share. People were so kind and loving. Most people had no idea how to relate, but every once in a while I would be with someone who had gone through the same thing. Funny how that happens.

You go through something like this and the Lord sends you people who can empathize and talk you through it. I also went through a frenzy of reading books about paranoid schizophrenics.

I really started to understand what my friend Karen had shared with me a year before. She told me from her own experience that this is not something you can get over. It follows you as long as the victim is living. Everything they go through touches you and affects your life. There were so many days of tears and disbelief. When Karen shared with me about her brother, she was trying to encourage me with her story. Her brother was diagnosed as a paranoid schizophrenic when he was 26. He lived until he was 40. He died homeless and alone in his car in California. She shared that those years from 26 to 40 were torment for her mother. She spent all her energy, money and time on him. She said it consumed her mom's life. Karen grabbed me by the shoulders, looked me in the eyes and said, "What James did not only destroyed his life, but could destroy yours as well. Now you are free to live your life as a living, breathing, healthy woman and know that James is at peace and in a much better place." She gave me a kiss. I was so grateful for what she shared because this was confirmation for what I truly believed the Holy Spirit was telling me about the future. This is why I could move forward, because what we have today is not all there is. There is eternity and that is what is more important than anything we value while on this earth. During the next two years, there was a lot of healing and grieving over James. I have to say there was some gratitude on my part that James didn't have to suffer for long on this earth, or hurt anyone else with the diagnosis he had. I kept thinking about my time in nursing school back in 1996 when we had our psych rotation. We were sent to Terrell State Hospital for five days. Each one of us was assigned a particular patient to observe and try to set up some sort of communication with. My patient was a 35-year-old male named Martin. His hair was matted, dirty and hung past his shoulders. His diagnosis was paranoid schizophrenia. As I observed him for a week and tried to set up a little bit of communication, I would listen to him rant and rave about the people coming to get him. Around the nurses' station, which was in the center of a big community room, there was a worn-out track in the carpet making a circle around the station. The patients would pace around this circle all day long. I was walking with Martin around the circle in order to try to get him to talk to me. Martin carried a Styrofoam cup with him and never set it down. It was dark brown on the inside. He told me, "They will poison me if I lay my cup down." Eventually after reading his charts and talking to some of his nurses, I found out a little about his past. He was born and raised in Dallas. He was very brilliant in math and his family were prominent people of Dallas. Beginning at age 19, he started having psychotic events and was in and out of mental facilities. When he was 23, he was in Russia. He got arrested because he was splashing naked in a large public fountain in the center of the town he was in. The irony being that I was given this particular patient at this time, while James was in his prime playing at home at the age of 10. No idea the road ahead of us.

In the weeks after James died, I went to visit with Chico at the Gaston House. He told me that it had really affected the guys at the house struggling with their sobriety. All of a sudden they got sober. I let them keep James' guitar as a memento of his time there. I am so grateful for the generosity of the Gaston House to take James in not knowing what lay ahead with him. My brother told me that he thought that James' incident did more to bring sobriety into those young men's lives than a thousand AA meetings would have.

A couple of weeks after James' death, I got a call from Baylor Hospital. They want to talk to me about James' surgery and his medical expenses. I was totally not ready for this. The lady was so sweet. She just said, "Ma'am, I just want to get James on Medicaid since he was basically an indigent. We can put him on Medicaid, if you will give me some information." I was taken aback for a minute, but then I thought, "Yes, he was basically an indigent." Kind of hard to take. I wrote an entry in my journal on October 12, 2010:

"I don't want to forget you, James! I keep thinking you are okay. You are at the Gaston House … plugging away. I always wondered how you 'really' were doing. Nobody knew. You hid it all so well on a day-to-day basis. Now that your body is gone, you are not wearing the Starbucks outfit. You are sitting with Jesus. I am so happy and at peace with that. Don't think that I have forgotten you as I just start living again in the world Jesus has put me in."

This is a "Note to James" that I wrote shortly after his death:

The enemy knew what an amazing young man you are before you were ever born. Your talents have blossomed and yet he wants them destroyed. The enemy pursued you and continually tried to destroy you, especially after the Holy Spirit touched your heart so deeply when you were 15 at your grandparents' evangelical service on their ranch in Breckenridge.

There was more pain than I could ever know or decipher. You were always the one to make others laugh, feel good and wanted, yet you obviously felt so lacking in that comfort. Your spiritual battles you were fighting alone. I truly believe you never knew who your enemy was.

It was not you.

You are irreplaceable, James. When you left this earth I'm sure you were greeted by your Papa, Grandma and Granddad. The love that Jesus has for you was wrapped all over you as you entered His presence. Finally, you are seeing the truth about you. You are loved and you are enough! You can do anything you choose to do. While you were here with us you would hesitate and sometimes simply refuse to try because I think you never felt like you were good enough. These were all lies the enemy was saying to you. I will see you again and smile as I imagine it! Because I know today you know the TRUTH! You are precious in His sight and beyond measure talented and able to conquer anything! This is a beyond heavenly perception!

I never could understand why life was so hard for you after you were 16 years of age. Divorce from my third husband occurred but you still had your friends up the street, who were like brothers. All my children had my love but I know that you were different in so many ways. I truly believe that your death was not your fault. It was another attempt to end your pain, the enemy's idea. As in all times in the past you knew you would "get fixed" and "be back." Just like the Gaston boys heard from you as they were rolling you into surgery on that fateful night.

"Hey guys, wait for me … I'll be back!"

After it was over and all the moments leading to that sorrowful day, it was God who was with me. I can remember feeling His loving arms wrapped around me when ML tried to pry me out of the pickup in the parking lot of Baylor Hospital Dallas. I kept telling him and sobbing uncontrollably that "If I get out of this truck and go up to that floor, I am admitting that James is dead, and I just can't do that!!"

The Lord wants to be with us in all our pain. He always holds our hand and sustains us when the pain is too great. You thought you were a mess, but I am a mess, we are ALL a "mess!" This is why we need God. What is God wanting to do in us through our mess? He isn't there to condemn us or keep letting us know how many times we blow it. He wants to bring us through and watch us flourish as it happens or after it happens. When all this is going on we don't really see it. Its only after it is all over that the art of the Lord shows us what we have learned.

We are His Masterpiece. God is always working on what's next in my life.

Surrender through it all. Give it to Him. He will hold you up when you aren't strong. There will be purpose in all our pain, either here or there.

Three weeks after James died I got the autopsy report from Baylor. Being a nurse, it was not hard to understand. His body was perfect except for his damaged heart and soul. Psalm 40:12 "For my heart has failed me and forsaken me." James' quote from one of his journals:

"Our hearts are green,
Our hearts are red,
Ours will stop
but we'll never be dead."

-James

CHAPTER 25

MISTY WATER-COLORED MEMORIES

*Therefore, we do not lose heart, but though the outer man
is decaying, yet our inner man is being renewed day by day.
For momentary, light affliction is producing for us an eternal
weight of glory far beyond all comparison, while we look not
at the things which are seen, but at the things which are not
seen; for the things which are seen are temporal, but the things
which are not seen are eternal.*

2 CORINTHIANS 4:16-18

The following are words that people shared about James after the funeral on the "RIP James Apple" Facebook page and through the funeral home condolences page:

Here is a classic story about James as told by one of his best buddies, Trey.

"It was New Year's Eve 2008. There was a NYE party at the Sheraton Hotel in downtown Dallas. There were about 15-20 of us that all got rooms at the hotel and tickets to the party they were having. After we all checked in and changed for the party that night, the plan was for everyone to meet down in the hotel lobby. It was a madhouse that night, being NYE, and nobody could find James in the lobby where we were supposed to meet because there were so many people. Well, after about 10 minutes of calling and texting and looking for James, he was not to be found. Then out of nowhere we hear the piano in the lobby start playing. It's James and he's playing "Shorty want a thug, bottles in the club" by Lil Wayne, which was a very popular song at the time. I thought for sure they would kick him off the piano, but instead everyone in the lobby, old people checking into the hotel, people working at the hotel and all our friends, all started singing along with James … only James could pull something off like that." *Trey S*

"There are no words to express my sympathy for the Apple family and all who knew James Apple. My memory is driving up to my house (we lived next door) and there he would sit with that contagious smile and his guitar at the end of his driveway just playing his music." *Kay B*

"Today when I was on my way to work, I was thinking about five years from now and how fun it would be to see and hang out with people from high school at our 10-year reunion. They were happy thoughts of future laughs looking back at what we used to be and celebrating who we had become. I pictured certain names and faces. I even looked forward to actually spending time with people I rarely spoke to. You see when I was in high school, for some reason, I didn't like myself. I didn't think anyone else liked me either, specifically the people I thought were 'cool.' There was a group of guys that I had gone to high school with since kindergarten, but by the time we got to high school I had convinced myself that I had no chance at being their friend, so instead I chose to avoid them. These guys were awesome. They were always the kids having the most fun. They were always laughing and making everyone around them smile. Even for wanting to avoid them these guys had a magnetism that drew people in and made people feel happy. They were the guys that were always there for each other. They were the guys I wanted to be more like. They were the guys I rarely spoke to. You see, it's been five years since we all graduated. It's been five years since I've seen most of them. I will get to see them all again and much sooner than I was thinking this morning on my way to work. We will all be at Fellowship Church in Dallas at 10 AM on Tuesday, but for a much less exciting occasion. As it turns out, we are not immortal. Today, the passing of James Apple has reminded us all of our mortality. We think about the future hoping and planning on great times with all those we know and love, yet we don't realize that at any given moment of any given day it can be taken from us that which we too easily take for granted. Facebook keeps us informed about what people are doing and we often substitute it for friendships themselves. Today on my way to work I had a choice. I could have called any one of the 100s of contacts in my phone that I could have been a better friend to. However, I refuse to regret my past decisions and instead I will strive to walk forward in a new and better way. I feel like I barely knew James, there were many of you out there who were much closer to him and you are all in my thoughts and prayers in this difficult time. I do, however, feel confident to say one thing about James. He had a gift, he had the ability to bring a smile to the most reluctant of faces. I once witnessed James even bring an angry teacher to . . . laughter in a matter of moments. So today as we sit here and remember James Apple, and realizing that our future plans will be different, let us do so in a way James would appreciate. Many of you have cried and will still cry. James, for me, was one of those guys I rarely spoke to, he was one of those guys I wanted to be more like. James was always able to make me laugh and smile. I would hope that we can all remember the love and joy that he so graciously shared with everyone. I will not remember him with tears in my eyes, I will remember him with once again a reluctant smile.

James loved music, and as I close I will challenge each of you. If you knew James better than me, if you knew James as little as me or if you didn't know James at all, I have a challenge for you.

Would you dare believe that you still have a reason to sing? Press on and just fight the good fight. Look forward to all the joyful moments that are still to come. Strive to celebrate each and every moment of each and every day. Enjoy those around you. Life is too short to avoid anyone. Life is too short to put things off till tomorrow. You never know what is around the corner, so celebrate where you are right now … even in the toughest moments."

RIP James Apple! *Jacob F*

"James didn't just play on the piano, he played it like he owned it. Nobody taught him how to play, he taught himself, but man did he play. He gave it his all, heart and soul were poured into pounding those 88s. He could make you laugh or bring tears to your eyes when he played ... but now there is silence where once was music and the tears in our eyes are there because the piano man is gone. We will sorely miss his smile, the way he tickled the ivories and the way he made us feel when we heard him play. This is dedicated to my friend James. We did not know each other for very long but he was my friend and I am glad that we had the chance to get to know one another. Rest in peace, my friend." *J. Sullivan*

"People come and go in our lives, some impress upon us while others just pass through with little remembrance. James was introduced to our family through our daughter, Crystal. When we first met James we knew immediately he was the kind of person who would make a lasting impression. He embraced the love of my family and we his. He spent many hours with us laughing, living and giving himself as only James Apple could do. His unselfish love even enabled him to bond with my mother-in-law who spoke no English. James' affectionate and unconditional love glowed towards 'Grandma,' as he called her. She affectionately referred to him as 'Little Boy.' James, we will miss you dearly, we will never forget you, thank you for the time you shared with my family, especially Crystal. May God welcome you home with all the Peace and Love you deserve." *P. Vasques*

"James always had the greatest smile and the ability to make all of us smile with him. We always told him he looked like our own garden gnome because of his rosy cheeks, round nose and his welcoming nature. He was a pleasure to work with and an incredible person to get to know." *Hope and Mike*

"I thought about you today, James. I'll never forget the truck that you had with the speaker on it. You used to make announcements with it in the school parking lot! LOL. Miss you!" *AB Baker*

"Well, I wasn't cool enough to know James that well, but I do remember once I was walking on Cooper Street and after recognizing me he yelled over the PA microphone he had on his truck. I was super embarrassed but he loved every minute of it and laughed even louder through the speaker! LOL. I wish there were more fun loving people with personalities like his in the world. I pray for strength and understanding for his grieving family ... specifically Tanson and Kolby." *Bo*

Lisa's song, "Jamie" written in 2007 and played at his funeral:

Jamie

Verse 1
Jamie come out and play It's another day lovely day
Can't you see we're here for you Don't you know you've got the truth You're holed up alone in your room
You look out the window when no one is looking at you
You may not be so alone
Some days I don't know

Chorus
Don't give up hope now
You'll find your way you're on the right side

Just keep movin' on We're all behind you now
Jamie, Jamie, Jamie

Verse 2
You always were the happy one
You smiled you laughed and had your fun
I guess we never heard your heart
And you never can tell when you smiled

Tag
We all grow, we all see
Life's not the picture we paint it to be But I got you and you
got me Jamie

2003 – Family trip to Nashville – Johnny, Uncle Russ and James on the "tour" bus

2003 – James leads ladies in Conga line at Wildhorse Saloon on Nashville trip

2005 – Lisa, Johnny and James having some fun

2006 – ML and I get married at Four Seasons, Irving, Texas

2009 – ML and I in Santorini, Greece

2010 – Lisa, Christy and Greg with James at
Pete's Dueling Piano Bar

2010 – James and I at Pete's before his performance

2010 – James playing at Pete's Piano Bar, Fort Worth, Texas

2010 – James' tombstone, Throckmorton Cemetery

2010 – ML and I with children of Baliet, Sudan

2010 – Rebekah and I walking together in Baliet, Sudan

*2011 – Me cheering the TCU Frogs to victory in
the Rose Bowl, Pasadena, California*

2011 – Me and best friend, Janice, with grandkids.
Whitaker (mine) and Riley (Janice's) at a TCU
home game in Fort Worth, Texas

2011 – Aunt Lisa with niece, Brinley, on family
beach vacation at Gulf Shores, Alabama

*2021 – Pops and KK with all the grandkids on
family vacation to Destin, Florida*

CHAPTER 26

OFF TO AFRICA

Things which eye has not seen and ear has not heard,
and which have not entered the heart of man, all that
God has prepared for those who love Him. For to us God
has revealed them through the Spirit; for the Spirit searches
all things, even the depths of God.

1 CORINTHIANS 2:9-10

In the ensuing days ahead, ML was busy getting ready to go on another South Sudan trip. This time, just about a week after James had died, ML sponsored a fundraiser at his studio for David Kaya, a native of South Sudan, who was very involved in starting churches all over South Sudan. ML had been asking me to think about going. I was very resistant. On the night of the meeting, I was watching and listening to David give his presentation. He showed pictures of the people who lived in the region. I saw their happy and contented smiles and then I saw their living conditions. They had been through a lot of war and torture in the past 10 years in Sudan with rebels trying to come and destroy them. Villages were being destroyed and the men killed, leaving the children and women to fend for themselves. A lot of these people became refugees and fled to Ethiopia and Uganda.

As David kept sharing, I started to get this feeling welling up inside of me, which I knew was the Holy Spirit. I realized that what I had to share with some of the women over there about losing my son might be a way to share the Lord with them. I started crying and ML came over and asked me, "What's wrong?" He probably thought I was crying about James because it would happen frequently for no reason, but this time I told him something different. I said, "I know you won't believe this but I believe that the Lord wants me to go share my story in South Sudan!" He stepped back and stared at me then gave me a big hug, actually with tears in his eyes. We went over and shared this with Mike, who was the leader of this mission. He was thrilled.

In a hustle, I had to get all my shots and get ready for this 12-day trip to "only my God knows where!" I had never been anywhere in Africa, much less a very undeveloped place. I was not afraid because I knew Who was calling me and Who was with me. I would go to all the team meetings to get prepared. The team was very interesting. There was a dentist going to help the people with dental issues. There were a total of four women and three men. One of the women was Carol, who was the funeral coordinator for James' funeral. I really had no idea what ML and I would be doing. The women were all business-oriented and they wanted to help the women learn how to start their own means of commerce in their communities.

On November 11, 2010, four weeks after James died, we flew from DFW Airport to Amsterdam where we had a four-hour layover. The only luggage we could take was a loaded-up backpack. Luckily, ML had just been on this journey a year ago so he knew what I should take. There were some meds we had to take and he liked to take his instant Starbucks coffee. I could only wear skirts or dresses, no pants for women. ML also told me to get a very comfortable, sturdy pair of walking shoes because we would be walking for miles every day. The place we were destined for was a small village called Baliet. There was a lot of Muslim influence in all of Africa, but in this village there were a lot of Catholics and nonbelievers.

From Amsterdam we flew to Uganda. From there we were going to get on a puddle-jumper plane to Juba, the capital of South Sudan. We spent the night in a little inn. The town was full of weapons. Soldiers were everywhere. We had to be careful not to take any pictures, which is always difficult for ML on trips, especially unusual ones like this trip. He would try to sneak some shots in, but our leader, Mike, told him no way or he would end up in jail. There was no electricity in our room, but there was a toilet. We didn't drink the water for obvious reasons. We had a million bottles of water for the entire trip. We went to a little place to eat and had beans with onions and tomatoes cooked with them. I remember some potatoes and some meat they called chicken, but I was skeptical. It certainly didn't look like any chicken I had seen in my lifetime. Sleep came easy that first night because we were exhausted from just getting there.

In the morning, we caught another small plane to Malekal, which was more backward than Juba. From there we got into a big Toyota SUV. There were two big SUVs full of our supplies for the week and all seven of us "missionaries." These trucks had all our tents, water bottles and camping essentials, plus our backpacks. Because it was so packed, I sat on the console between the driver and passenger seat up front where ML sat. The rest of the team was in the SUV behind us.

Off we went, heading to Baliet, which was only about 50 miles away from Malekal. I thought, "This shouldn't take too long," as I sat bouncing on the hard console. We traveled down the most dusty and potholed dirt roads I have ever seen. We bounced in the car with our heads hitting the ceiling at times. All along the way, I was observing the truckloads of armed soldiers carrying assault weapons and looking very angry. It was a scary ride. At one point, a patrol stopped us and they spoke Arabic to our driver. It took a while for him to release us to drive on. The temperature was in the low 90s for most of our time in South Sudan. It is very close to the equator. We came during their dry season so we could get around the village and do what we came to do, versus the rainy season where most of the time we would be drenched. The SUV had no air-conditioning, so besides being very cramped we were hot. I started to feel a bit claustrophobic with the heat and the cramped seating arrangements. I remembered this had only happened to me once before. When I was single, I had gone to Las Vegas with some girlfriends. On our return trip the airplane was told to sit on the tarmac to wait for a gate. It was about 117 degrees on the tarmac. There was no cool air circulating in the cabin. I was sitting between two large men and the clock was ticking. I got that same claustrophobic feeling I was having in the SUV. I did just what I did when I was sitting on that tarmac. I prayed for calm from the Holy Spirit and picked something ahead of me to stare at. I chose to stare at the dusty, potholed road ahead. It truly seemed to calm me down. Fortunately, I never did have to yell to stop the car!

What I thought would be about a two-hour drive ended up being a four-hour ride. All along the way, we went through several villages. The houses were called tukuls. They were circular huts with mud and grass roofs and sides. There were campfires outside of the huts with women and children tending to their cooking fires. Children were running everywhere. The terrain was dry and parched and extremely dusty. There was no hint of any prosperity or verdant areas. All dry and arid, lots of dust and very few trees.

We eventually drove into the village of Baliet. The children were noisily and excitedly running to our SUVs to greet us. We came to the area of the village where Pastor John, a native Sudanese, and his little church lived. The drivers of the SUVs helped to unload us and helped to pitch all the tents. As I took all this in, I thought, "I am actually in a third-world country … no running water, no electricity and no plumbing." The village women went down to the river that ran through the village to collect the water. They carried large plastic barrels on their heads full of river water. As we got oriented to the area where we would be for eight days, David Kaya, who headed up the local mission we were on, would point out the shower area and the toilet area. All these areas were covered and made private. It consisted of barrels of water on elevated poles where you get under and pull a rope to make the water rain down on you. He told us not to open our mouth while in the shower. I thought to myself, that should be really easy considering that I saw the source of that water. Also, he showed us the toilet. It was a hole in the ground in a tent. There was toilet paper sitting on the dirt floor. There was dirt everywhere. They told us that the small local church women would be preparing our meals over the big campfire three times a day. He also warned us to drink as much bottled water as we could, because the sun was very intense and we would be out in it all day. There was very little shade in Baliet.

ML and I settled into our tent and got it organized. Mike called a meeting to discuss our mission there. He told ML and me that all he wanted us to do was go from hut to hut and share our story of meeting Jesus and what He had done for us. He also told us that most of the villagers will say yes when asked if they are Christians. They were born into the Catholic Church and really didn't understand what being "born again" meant. So he wanted us to talk to them about the person of Jesus and what a joy it is to "know Him." Matthew was going to be our interpreter every day for the whole eight days of our stay. When we met him, I found him to be a joy. He was friendly and truly had a servant's heart. I knew we would enjoy being with him, and his English was excellent!

As we went to "tent" the first night after our orientation, I felt really organized and thought we would be as comfortable as possible considering the circumstances. We kissed goodnight as we lay on top of our sleeping bags and told the Lord how grateful we were for His protection and guidance throughout our arrival. Aah, to sleep. Don't ask me the time because I never knew what time it was in South Sudan. It was either daylight or nighttime or breakfast, lunch or dinner!

Well, that first night, we woke up from a torrent of rain coming through the top of our tent. When it rains there, it is huge. We were deluged with rainwater and everything we had was soaking wet. We just sat in our tent until morning because there was really nothing we could do to fix it until daybreak. Once daybreak hit, the crew saw that they had forgotten to put the rain guard on top of our tent, so there you go! All was corrected and of course we had plenty of days left in Baliet for our belongings to be dried out. Nobody told us that tenting skills were a requirement.

Our first morning in Baliet was wonderful, despite the rainout we incurred! I am a big morning tea drinker. I love any kind of hot tea, herbal or black. We came to the ladies' campfire and sat in our white PVC chairs. Of course we were still soaking wet and all our other friends were dry asking questions about what had happened to us during the night. Naturally there were laughs to go all around, including us! ML had his Starbucks instant coffee so all he needed was hot water. They brought me Lipton teabags and hot water. Which was amazing! Then they brought us what was the total equivalent of New Orleans "beignets!" They were to die for. They really could be in a four-star New Orleans hotel if they had just looked a little more appetizing. They knew how to take the rudimentary ingredients of beignets, lots of sugar and *voilà!* What a wonderful first-day surprise. I closed my eyes and just depended on my sense of smell and taste.

I was excited for the challenge to share with these new friends, but inside I knew that they really could not relate to me, a white woman from America. I felt like I was just something curious for them to look at. George W. Bush was president when we were there and the consensus among the South Sudanese was that he was for the new South Sudanese to become their own nation, away from Sudan, controlled by Bashir and the Muslim government. In fact, when we walked through the little village of Baliet and met the men, both young and old, they would be lounging around and chanting George W. Bush's name like he was their "savior." In the meantime, the women could be found laboring over the campfires and cleaning the clothes by the river.

Their hope was that their new President Kiir would be able to break the shackles with Sudan and they could become a free and independent nation. He even had a cowboy hat George W. Bush gave him that he wore all the time to prove to his nation George W. Bush's promises were going to bring South Sudan's independence. They were depending on him to fund this new government. I had seen that these people were very dependent on someone else to take care of them and there was little self-initiative in them. I had a hard time believing that independence was going to work for them. I continued with our mission not to talk about the political atmosphere, but to show them that there was "A GOD IN HEAVEN." This God could change your heart and your attitudes about this temporal life we live on this earth.

As ML and I would go to share "our stories" with mostly women on the outskirts of the village, we could see that since all the men were gone to the village or out in the fields tending their cattle, this was going to be a women's ministry. I was ready! I began to share my story about losing my son in the prior month and there was a definite uptick of interest when I told them that my son had died a month earlier. A lot of these women had lost husbands, daughters and sons to the rebels who had invaded South Sudan. We had an entourage of women and children who followed us throughout the area.

In the first couple of days we would just rotate around the village of Baliet. We would gather around campfires with the women and children. I would tell them Bible stores. It was kind of like vacation Bible school, only in Africa! Thank You, Lord, we had Matthew to translate or we would have been helpless. Our leader, Mike, had told us to only go into areas where we felt the Holy Spirit leading us. The women we approached were mostly responsive and I got to share stories and some of my testimony. We did come to one large compound with a mother, three older sons and lots of children. As we approached the campfire, I could feel the spirit of resistance and I told ML that we should move on, but we went on in to talk a little with the people there. After very little conversation I could tell that there was a Satanic resistance to us being there and we quickly left. It was very creepy. In America, there is a numbness to the spiritual realm, the holy and the evil. We are so focused on the material and have our five senses trained to translate all we experience. We mostly ignore or don't even consider that there may be another realm to reality. Therefore, most Americans don't sense the evil that truly does exist in this world. When you go away to a place like Africa, where spirit worship and black magic are prolific, there is definitely a different realm of reality that one has to recognize. As ML and I were walking around these tukuls, the people who would walk up to us and welcome us seemed to be of the light. There were those who would shirk away from us and hide their faces and you could sense the darkness in their spirit.

Our interpreter, Matthew, suggested to us that we go to a village that was a little farther away from Baliet to share our story and Bible stories. So out we trekked about an hour's walk away to another small village with some beautiful trees. As we approached the area, the children were everywhere. It seemed like the reception Jesus would receive when he would be welcomed into a village. The children would see us coming and they would gather the white PVC chairs and place them under the tree. There was a lot of excitement and shouting. Of course, ML had his camera out and was taking lots of pictures and showing the children and adults their pictures right after taking them. There was a lot of laughter with that because I don't believe that any of those children or adults had ever seen their actual image. Once he took a picture of an old woman in Baliet sitting next to her campfire. She just caught ML's eye. We went and spoke to her and all she did when Matthew would translate was just giggle. She was very old and had few teeth left. Matthew asked her if ML could take her picture. Of course she nodded yes because I don't even think she knew what that meant. He took the picture and told Matthew to ask her if she wanted to see it. She nodded. ML showed her the pictures of herself and she laughed so hard the whole village heard her. Someone in our group told us that some of these young children had never laid eyes on a white person, much less had their picture taken.

We started going every day to this particular village on the hill under the big tree where all the women and children would show up. I can actually see some of their faces in my mind's eye. Our leader, Mike, had told us to reach out and connect to those in the villages we believed were the leaders, male or female. We were on day two in this particular village. I started sharing my stories like I had been doing. I was telling Bible stories about God's power, His protection and His love. I was just telling stories, like I used to do with my kids. Thank goodness I had Matthew to interpret. I would try to interject some humor to get the little ones to laugh, which wasn't hard to do. These women and children were so happy and joyous. On the third day, we were doing our Bible stories. I saw a beautiful woman walking toward our circle with some young women surrounding her. I watched the way she approached. I saw how the younger women gave her a white PVC chair up front next to mine. I knew that I had the ear of the women's village leader. She looked like a leader and held herself like one. She sat and I continued to tell the stories to the children.

After I was done, she came over to ask me through our interpreter what I was doing and where I was from. Through Matthew, I shared my story of where I was from and why I was there. I didn't share anything about James yet, only about our mission. She was so beautiful. Her name was Rebekah. After that day, that is all I learned about her. She left but I did tell her we would be back at the same time the next day. The Lord had shown me my mission in Africa. Her name was Rebekah. I shared it with Mike, our leader, and he was thrilled. He just encouraged us to keep making the hour walk to spend the day with them. This is what we did every day until we left. Matthew was so amazing. How little these interpreters know about how valuable their work is in connecting two spirits. Even more than that.

So for the next five days ML and I would head out to see Rebekah on the hill under the tree. All the children and young women would show up before we even got there. The children would have the white PVC chairs set up so we could sit and the kids would sit at our feet on the ground. You could see them preparing for our arrival as we walked up the hill to the tree. After a few days, I told Matthew that I wanted to have a private session with Rebekah. He asked Rebekah and she agreed. I could feel that we had a strong connection. We had a quiet talk together on the next day. This was when I shared with her about losing my son one month earlier. She tells me her story.

She was only 18 years old in the late eighties. The rebellion in South Sudan was getting so bad that every man she knew was getting swallowed up in the rebellion army. The women and girls were being raped and tortured. She just wanted to leave. She escaped out of her village and ended up north in Khartoum. She thought that she would be safe there. She got an apartment with another girl and a job in a factory. She was pregnant at the time, but told no one because she was afraid she would lose her job and be kicked out of her apartment. She kept going to work and ended up delivering her baby in her apartment alone. Her baby survived delivery and Rebekah would nurse her whenever she could. Her work became more strenuous. She eventually could no longer go home to care for her infant enough during the long day shift. Her baby died from lack of feeding. She was devastated and so lost. My heart totally went out to her. She told me that she had not had any children since she moved back to this village. She was hoping to have another family whenever they would have a free and independent country from Sudan. It was going to be called South Sudan.

I shared with Rebekah about my James, his struggles and his death. She was so kind and sympathetic. I think the main thing we had in common was a mother's love. I shared with her and her whole village of women about the love of Christ and the new life that He gives which frees us from fear of death. This is a message that the people who live under these harsh regimes need to hear as well as all of humanity. This life is not all there is. There is so much more than what we see with our eyes and senses. There is the eternal and the immortal. This is what we are. Why do we fear? We have so much more to live for. I know truly that she, by the end of our trip, got it. When we had our last day on the hill, there were about 20 kids from Rebekah's village who wanted to get baptized. ML and Matthew baptized them in the local river, more like a small swamp.

ML had heard there were snakes in that river, but bless his heart, he walked down into it and baptized all these kids with no fear of what might lurk under the surface. He was safe in the care of his Heavenly Father. What a glorious day! Rebekah and I were on the sidelines watching the whole thing! Not a single snake was seen!

Once our trip came to a close and we were getting all packed up to leave, a messenger came to our leader, Mike, and whispered into his ear. Mike had a rather solemn look on his face and gathered all of us together to share the news with us. "We are going to have to put off our leaving for a few hours because there is some rebel activity down the road we have to travel on to get out." We were all caught off guard with this news. In the meantime, while we waited we began to pray that the Lord would protect us and get us out safely so we would be able to catch our puddle-jumper plane in Malekal and get to Juba. It was a bit scary to be in this third-world country and get that kind of news. Our supplies were low and it was time to go home. We were all trusting the Lord to get us out. After about an hour, another messenger came and told us that he thought we could leave safely. We loaded up in the cramped SUVs and said our goodbyes to all the village, especially all the children. Off we went into the unknown. We were all vigilantly in prayer for safety, mercy and grace with the rebels who were ahead on our road. We passed several posts of rebels with their AK-47s in their arms. At every outpost we were waved ahead with the rebels giving us a good staring as we passed by. Several hours later, we were approaching Malekal and were so grateful to have made it safely to this destination.

We got to the airport in time and were basking in the fact of God's protection in this hostile environment. We made it to Juba and then eventually we were in Kampala, Uganda, where we spent the night in a sort of jungle hotel. We had electricity and plumbing.

We were so grateful. We eventually made it home to Dallas with a wonderful "Welcome Home" greeting by all the grandkids with their posters and all! Never ever have I been so grateful to be back in the "Good Ole US of A!" We would keep up with the news of South Sudan. As the people there had hoped, in 2011 South Sudan became an independent nation from Sudan. But since then wars have broken out again and our small village of Baliet and Rebekah's village are gone. Most of the people who have survived live in refugee villages in Uganda and Somalia. Many people have died. Our friend Mike has said he has not heard any news about Rebekah, but I choose to believe that the Lord has protected her and her family throughout this mess.

CHAPTER 27

LIFE GOES ON

Weeping may last for the night,
but a shout of joy comes in the morning.
PSALM 30:5

I would have despaired unless I had believed that
I would see the goodness of the Lord in the land of the living.
Wait for the Lord; be strong, and let your heart
take courage; Yes, wait for the Lord.
PSALM 27:13-15

When we got home, it was time to start getting ready for Christmas. I knew this would be a very difficult Christmas for our whole family. My sister, Cheryl, volunteered to host the family event in her large home. Our family continued growing and by then some of the cousins had gotten married and were having babies. There was a gloomy cloud over the day because the one who always entertained us during holidays was gone and never coming back. We had tears and some people shared about their feelings from losing James. He was dearly missed, but I truly believe that by this time all of us knew of the misery he was going through before his death. It truly helps to get through the grief when you have so many loved ones around you who are sharing this with you. I am grateful for all the cousins, aunts, uncles and Mama and Papa who James had around him. We all tried in one way or another to help him out. Family will always be there for you through it all.

In the years following James' death, I struggled with the grief and loss, but thanks to my Heavenly Father I can honestly say I never felt guilty about James' death. I spoke with several women whose names were given to me who had lost a young adult child to suicide. All I could share was what I experienced. When you are walking by faith through anything difficult and are truly trusting God to be there with you through it all, there is a calm and rest that is hard to find if that is not the case.

When I would share with some of the parents, they truly had a hard time with that concept. Sometimes I would think that they thought that you "had" to feel guilty if your child did something to destroy their life. I will always remember what the doctor at JPS told me as she grabbed my hand, "This is not your responsibility. I release you from this! It is not your fault!"

Many times I would write letters to James talking about how I was feeling and telling him that he would always be in my heart. I so looked forward to the day when I would see him again in his happy-go-lucky self that I clearly remember from his childhood. During this period I also gained a lack of fear about death. I knew that there would be a day that would come and it would be my time to go. I really had no fear or remorse because to me it would be a truly happy day to see all those whom I had cried over when they left here but will rejoice to see them again. Life goes on and on and on! This is our heritage as believers if we truly will believe that this is God's plan for us. He wants us to have a longing for the eternal. "He has made EVERYTHING appropriate in its time and He has also set eternity in man's heart" (Ecclesiastes 3:11). When this happens in our hearts, the mortal and the temporary things in this world become subservient to this wonderful freeing truth of the eternal and immortal.

CHAPTER 28

MY SWEET JANICE

Every good thing bestowed and every perfect gift is from
above, coming down from the Father of lights, with whom
there is no variation or shifting shadow. In the exercise of
His will He brought us forth by the word of truth, so that
we might be, as it were, the first fruits among His creatures.

JAMES 1:17-18

In February 2012, I turned 60 years old! ML and I had been married for six years by then. It is a fun and sweet marriage.

No games, no agenda, just sweet and uncomplicated love and kindness. I was so grateful for life to be GOOD! Unbeknownst to me, ML, my kids and some friends were planning a super surprise party for "KK." KK became my grandma name after my first grandchild was born in 2005. Before he was born, I told Christy that I wanted my Grandma name to be "Honey" because I had seen a video of one of my dear friend's granddaughter calling her "Honey." It melted my heart. Christy let me know, in no uncertain terms, that the name "Honey" was not acceptable! She asked me to think of another one. The only other nickname I could remember when growing up was KK. My brother, Russell, started calling me that when he started to talk, so I guess it stuck because I got the daughter approval on that. So "KK" I became in 2006 and it has pretty much stuck with almost everyone I know. The surprise birthday plan was that we were going to meet the kids up at the club for birthday dinner that night. This was no surprise because this is where we celebrated a lot of family events. I never did have any kind of suspicion about the party. Once we got to the club, I took a minute getting out of the car because I had forgotten to put in my hearing aids. As ML was opening the door for me, I noticed him looking around the parking lot, but I didn't think anything about it. Once we reached the door to the club I saw my oldest grandson, Whitaker, opening the door and kind of escorting us in. He told me that we were going to eat in a different area than the place I assumed we would go. He led us down a hallway and someone from inside the big ballroom opened the doors and everyone yelled "Surprise!" as we walked in with Whit. I was so shocked and truly surprised. I was laughing and crying at the same time. I have never been given a surprise party before. I just started laughing and asking a million questions. "How did you pull this off, who did all this?" So many people were there. The ballroom was full! Relatives, friends, high school friends, college friends, so much love and excitement. They were so excited that I was really surprised. I think half the fun of a surprise party is not for the recipient but for the people hosting the party to know that they really did pull off a great surprise. They truly did and I could tell everyone was having so much fun! Hugs around for everyone. There was so much love and I felt very blessed by the wonderful people God had put in my life. But not all my important birthdays turned out so wonderfully in the past. God is so wonderful in restoring the good things back to us. Now that my 70th birthday is coming up, I will keep my eyes and ears open. My precious TCU friends, Janice and Josh, had started to become a bigger part of ML's and my life around 2009. ML and I had gotten TCU season tickets and the Frogs were having some awesome seasons, winning a lot under Coach Patterson. We would tailgate with the Janice and Josh crowd and have a great time. Also Janice and I had started seeing each other a lot more. I really was sad that we lost so many years during the eighties. But my life was pretty chaotic and that kind of thing was off the radar for me. So when my life settled down and I was single again in 2003 we got together. We decided it was time for us to make up for lost time. We enjoyed golf, eating out and traveling places together. I truly saw Janice as "closer than a sister." Once ML and I married, Janice and Josh really did like ML so we started seeing them more together. We had bought our home in White Bluff near Whitney, Texas in 2010 before James died. We had remodeled some of the house and were ready to have friends and family come and spend the weekend to relax, eat and play golf. I couldn't count how many times that Janice and Josh would come to stay. Our White Bluff guests grew to include other TCU friends: Ed and Susan, Gary and Sharlotte, who became regulars. They loved to come down when TCU had an away game. We would watch the game then play golf and talk forever on the patio. Starting at the end of 2010 after James died, we could see that

White Bluff would be our God-given treasure to share with as many friends as we could ask. It is a magical and beautiful spot. Needless to say, I cannot even tell you how many people have walked through the threshold of this blessed home. We have had family reunions, volleyball teams with coaches, baseball teams, soccer teams, TCU friends, all kinds of family, golfing girlfriends, and Christian retreats. It has been wonderful, and only GOD could have foreseen that during the horrible year of 2010 this family would need a beautiful and peaceful spot to heal, refresh and connect. My grandkids have grown up here during spring breaks and summer vacations.

I want to pay tribute to my wonderful dad, because without him we would have none of this. In 2007, he starting giving my sister, brother and me money that he had accumulated. Trusts were set up. Through all this each one of us kids has been so blessed to bless our own families with Dad's fortune. When we bought White Bluff, I was able to pay for most of it through his generosity. I have always believed that because we did have to move so much that Dad always wanted us to know that he was sorry for moving and uprooting us so much growing up. I kind of think this was his way of saying "I'm sorry, go and enjoy the fruits of my labor." Have we ever! Because of my dad I have taken all my kids on wonderful vacations and we are blessed with White Bluff. Having a loving and generous father is truly a great blessing. So every time I am at White Bluff with a houseful of friends, who always tell me that "White Bluff is such a blessing," I just look up to heaven and say, "Thanks, Dad."

On November 4, 2016, the whole TCU gang was here for a TCU football watching party and golf as usual. I remember because Janice and Josh gave me a wonderful devotional book with a sweet note in the front signed by both of them. I still read it to this day when I'm here at White Bluff. On the evening of November 14, 2016, only 10 days since we had shared that fun-filled weekend together, I got a tearful call from Josh. The first words out of his mouth were, "Kay, Janice is dead!" I couldn't believe what I was hearing. He started to explain what happened to her and how her body was destroyed in a huge car accident on Interstate 30 heading to their lake house in Greenville. Her car was stopped because of an accident in front of her and a semi-truck going 70 miles per hour rear-ended her stopped car. It crushed her and the car beyond recognition. The car exploded into a huge fireball. Janice was gone instantaneously. I was dumbfounded and could not quit crying for several days. We went to see Josh in Fort Worth to see how he was, and he seemed to be taking the accident well. He shared with us that before she left for Greenville they had just talked about who was going to go first. She told Josh that she wanted to be the one to go first because she didn't think she could manage without Josh around. She even told Josh that if anything happened to her first that he would have her blessing to get married again. Josh blew all this off until the next day, as he was at home waiting for Janice to return from Greenville. His doorbell rang. The sheriff and a DPS officer were at his front door to break the news. My sweet sister in the Lord is with my sweet baby James and with her loving Lord. Knowing this makes all believers have such a peace knowing that their loved ones are complete, not in pain. Janice, I love you and know that you are so content. I'm sure you are smiling down at Josh as you always did when you were here.

CHAPTER 29

SURPRISE FAMILY

Now to Him who is able to do exceedingly abundantly beyond all that we ask or think, according to the power that works within us, to Him be the glory in the church and in Christ Jesus to all generations forever and ever. Amen.

EPHESIANS 3:20-21

My oldest daughter, Christy, has continued since early 2000 to keep up with her other grandmother Eunice, who is Steve's mother. She told me that they were friends on Facebook. She never says anything about her biological dad. Christy and Greg have four children and are living the suburban life close to me.

As a large family, we started in 2011 going on family beach vacations every year. On our trip to Port Aransas in 2018, the grandkids and ML had all gone to bed, and it was just me and my three children, Christy, Lisa and Johnny, and my daughter-in-law, Katie. I really don't remember how the conversation started but there were some questions about my life.

I proceeded to share with them some about my marriage to Steve. They were a captive audience. Katie, especially, was so surprised at the story. She would comment, "I had no idea all that happened and how did you survive it all?" My only answer to that question is, "The grace of God is so good! Only by His love, mercy and grace do I still have my sanity!" As the night went on, we came up with a new trip we felt that we needed to take. We decided that we would fly to Nashville to sightsee and go see their cousin Wesley, his wife and three girls. Christy, her kids and I were going to take a side trip to Chattanooga to see Eunice. She would also get to meet her four great-grandkids. Christy really wanted to do this. I got excited about it and a little hesitant all at the same time. I had always liked Eunice despite all the pain and chaos before and after Christy was born.

In August 2018, all 12 of us boarded a Southwest plane headed to Nashville, Tennessee. I am a true fan of Nashville. Lisa's years at Belmont University were my excuse to go there and enjoy it all. We had a wonderful and fun-filled time enjoying all the sights and sounds of Nashville. We had rented a huge Mercedes van. There was room for all and even more room for dancing in the van, which Johnny did several times when Christy, our van driver, would put on the rap music! Wild and crazy with lots of fun and memories galore.

After a few days of visiting in Nashville, Christy, the kids and I headed to Chattanooga to see Eunice, whom I had not seen since 1974 at Steve's and my wedding in Houston, Texas. Christy had been to see Eunice after she graduated from Texas Tech. She took some business trips to Florida where Eunice was living at the time. Eunice, in the meantime, had moved from Florida to Chattanooga to be near her youngest son and Steve's younger brother, Paul. I remembered Paul. I really liked him. He was sweet, outgoing and the kind of guy who made you feel at ease and liked. I was kind of excited to see him again after all these years.

I was getting butterflies as we drove to Eunice's house. She met us at her front door. Naturally she was thrilled to hug and meet all her new great-grandkids. She was already familiar with each one of them because Christy had shared so much about them with her on Facebook. As we walked through her house, I saw pictures of Steve, his sister Marty and other family photos on the walls. She told me she rarely saw either of them. I really didn't ask many questions, just listened, taking it all in. We were going to meet Paul for dinner that night. We met him at a nearby restaurant and I have to say it was a joy to see him again after 44 years. There was a sweet rapport between all of us. There wasn't any feeling of bitterness or animosity. I kept thinking what a blessing for us to meet and reacquaint for the sake of the grandkids to know more about all their family, even if it is a little unusual to say the least. The evening was nice and felt good all around as we left to go back to our hotel. The next day we did some sightseeing in Chattanooga, which has a lovely downtown and lots of sights to take in. That night we were going to have dinner with Eunice, Paul, his wife and daughter. We ended up having a great time together, but never a word was mentioned about Steve. That's the only part of all this that I thought was strange. But if they didn't want to talk about any of it, then I was cool with that.

We all said our goodbyes and went back to our hotel. The next day we headed back to Nashville to pick up Lisa at some friends' house and get on the plane back to Dallas. As I reflected on these events, I just wanted to bless my daughter for being so sweet to reconnect to the grandmother she never got to meet until later on in life. I also wanted to thank the Lord for placing a sweet connection between me, Eunice and Paul. I'm sure my grandkids benefited tremendously from the honesty and openness in that relationship, maybe not now but definitely when they get older and have experienced more of what life has in store for them. There won't be the secrets that cause so much distrust in families. I always think it is better to go forward, forgive and be honest than to try to cover up things you might think are not normal. Let me just say, "Who and what is 'normal' anyway?"

After this visit, Christy started hearing from Steve's son, Parker, unbeknownst to me. He had graduated from the University of Virginia a couple of years before and had gotten a job in Dallas around 2018. I didn't know that she had connected with him until Christmas 2019. She casually told me that her half-brother, Parker, was coming to Christmas at Johnny's house. I said, "OH!" I had no idea that she had been inviting him to come watch her team's volleyball games and he had met all her kids. Apparently, when he graduated from University of Virginia, he moved to Dallas to work, and his grandmother, Eunice, had put him in touch with Christy. He really didn't know anyone in Dallas. Christy was so friendly and open to letting him into her world. I'm sure he was glad to be around her and her kids.

That Christmas was quite a day. Parker came in and I had no idea what a big guy he was. He is six foot five and looked like a college football player, towering over us all. He had been on a football scholarship at University of Virginia. He fit right in and was outgoing and friendly. He reminded me a lot of his uncle Paul. I talked to him a little about his dad and his family. He told me that he does not talk to or see his dad very frequently. His dad and mom had been divorced for quite some time after the death of his older sister from heart issues when she was in her early twenties. I told him I was so glad that he came and connected with us. As I looked at Parker from a distance, I was shocked at how much he looked like his dad and how much he looked like Christy.

Before we sit down to eat, we usually get in a big circle where we are all holding hands. Each one of us shares what they are thankful for. It is so precious, especially to hear the younger ones. On this day, when it was Parker's turn, without any shyness, he told us all that he was so grateful to have found us and he felt right at home with us. It is rather like quantum physics. There is never any space once you have touched someone. Even though Parker's dad and I are apart, he is still part of the circle. What a wonderful thing that my ex-husband's child is becoming a part of my family. When I sat down to visit with him I kept thinking, "What a shame that your dad couldn't be as social and free as you are." This connection just proves that future generations should not have to take on their ancestors' mistakes. Future generations should not pay for your choices and bad judgment. Since then, Parker has come to all our Christmases and Thanksgivings. This year he also came to our Easter dinner. He and I got into a great discussion and

I took a bunny trail in my mind. "If I was still married to your dad it would be 47 years gone by and you could have been my son." He is a precious man and my prayer for him is to find a wonderful woman he loves who will embrace with all of us this craziness we call "life." Life is strange and stranger still when you are open-minded and open-hearted to whatever it brings your way.

Also at most of our family events is John Apple's son, Josh. Lisa has always kept an eye on Josh, since he is her and Johnny's much younger half-brother. She has loved and mentored him, especially since he was so young when John died. That first Christmas when Parker showed up, Josh also was there. One big happy family! What is so great is that we really do have a blast together with loving acceptance of all who show up. That is one important fact about living a great life – just show up!

One of the most recent God moments in my life where I showed up and so did He happened in October of 2019. ML and I had planned a trip to Washington, DC to tour and attend a seminar put on by a Black conservative woman, Star Parker. We have been supporting her cause to help the American Black population get out from under the heavy un-helpful hand of Uncle Sam. Her organization's goal was for the Black community to gain the God-given abilities God has for them so they can do a job well and profit from their labors, not always taking the dole from the government. She is a very active promoter along with a lot of her protégées. We were excited about our political agenda and our tourist agenda on this trip. We had boarded our Southwest plane and picked out our seats. ML, being six foot four, always liked the aisle seat. Being the window-watcher I am, I always got the window seat. This always left the middle seat empty. Naturally this gave me the excitement of wondering who the Lord would place between us on a flight. As we were settling in, I saw the crowd passing by us and wondered who would take this seat. I saw a middle-aged woman with salt-and-pepper hair pass by. She kept going. A little later I saw her come back to our aisle. She asked ML if the seat was taken. ML said no. She sat down and got settled. I said hi and introduced myself and ML. I could tell she thought it was strange that we weren't sitting together but I told her that our preferences for aisle and window seats was our excuse. On most planes we have to sit together but not today. She introduced herself as Ruth and she lived in Grand Prairie.

Once the plane got in the air, she asked me why we were going to DC. I told her about Star Parker and a little of our itinerary. When I asked her the same question, she told me that she was going to the Holocaust Museum. I told her we were too. Then I asked her why was she only going there. "To do more research about my family," she replied.

Well, that answer totally lit me up and I was ready with a million questions. Poor Ruth, she had no idea what she was in for. Over the past three years my book club had become prolific in reading books written about the Holocaust and all the tragic personal stories that went along with that horrible time in history. She told me that she was going to spend the week with a historian who works at the museum to help Jewish families find information about their lost loved ones. I was totally fascinated to know that right before me was a real person who actually had relatives who survived the genocide of the Jewish population of Europe at Hitler's hands. I explained to her my strong interest in her endeavors of trying find out more about her relatives killed during the war. I told her about my TCU trip to Europe and how fascinated I was traveling through Europe and imagining how different European life was back during the war. I shared with her about Corrie Ten Boom's clock shop and the book *The Hiding Place*. But enough about me, I had a zillion questions to ask her. She was so open to sharing with me and as a result we talked nonstop the whole three-hour flight.

Ruth told me that her mother and father were Jews in Poland in the forties. When Hitler invaded Poland, they were eventually sent to concentration and work camps in Germany and Poland. Her mother and father didn't even know each other during that horrible time of their lives. She had an aunt who was still alive in Florida. She was also in the camps and eventually got out and came to America. What was so interesting about her parents was that after the war and their release from the camps, as fate would have it, they both ended up in Fort Worth, Texas in the early fifties, met and got married. Ruth was raised in Fort Worth and has lived in the Dallas/ Fort Worth area her whole life. Our conversation branched out to her childhood and teenage years. I wondered what her parents were like and if they talked about the war. I asked her what her dad told her when the topic of the Holocaust came up in her history classes in high school and she told me that he told her, "We don't EVER talk about it to anyone." She said that they never spoke of it to her either. I found Ruth to be a wonderful, open, friendly and warm person whom I wanted to get to know. She told me all about her life, her careers and her multitude of hobbies. She is a very creative person. When she was finally able to ask me a few questions about myself, the inevitable question of children came up. I told her about my kids and shared my story about James. Whenever I get asked about my kids, I have to be discreet depending on who is asking. If the person is not really interested and I probably won't see them ever again, I just say three, but most of the time I do tell that I have three living here and one in heaven. But with Ruth, I could tell she wanted to talk about James and my experiences with him and his illness. As God would arrange, before we landed she was sharing with me about her husband and his severe depression and what a burden it is for her and their marriage.

After listening to Ruth and her listening to me for three hours, we knew that this was not a one-time deal. I got her contact information and told her I would call her when we were back home and we would meet for lunch. After we got off the plane, I told her I would pray for her and her search for her relatives. ML and I thoroughly enjoyed every minute of our DC trip. Once we got to the Holocaust Museum, I found myself seeing it all from a different perspective since I actually got to see it through the eyes of a child of survivors. I still know that there is so much pain I could never know from being the child of two people who endured such tragedies during the Nazi captivity. Seeing her parents suffer later in life from their pain and loss from being the object of such human hatred was such a tragedy for all of Ruth's family. All they were trying to do was create a life here in America and have true freedom. Once we got back home, I couldn't quit thinking about Ruth and I would share her story with a lot of my friends and family.

In February 2020, prior to the COVID lockdown, Ruth and I met for lunch in Irving. It was so good to see her again. Right after we were seated at our table, she immediately told me that her husband, who had depression really bad, had shot and killed himself with his shotgun shortly after she returned from DC. I was stunned. She proceeded to tell me the whole story.

She was the one who found him dead in his bedroom after she had gone to pick up take-out lunch one day. She was totally caught off guard. Needless to say, our lunch lasted way into the afternoon. I knew then that the Lord had truly brought us together on that airplane for a lot of reasons. We continue to see each other and share the good and the bad. We got together during the lockdown around November 2020 and again in the spring of 2021. She has truly been a woman who has flourished during her life despite all the setbacks. I share the Lord with her and all that He has meant to me during all my ordeals. So now, of course, she is excited to read all about it in my story. Ruth has done so much research on her family prior to and during the war that she has created a presentation that she gives to small groups. I had her come to speak to a social group of women that Janice got me involved in prior to her death. I shared Ruth with these ladies and they were thrilled. You could tell that hearing from someone who had firsthand experience with the Holocaust survivors was a rare experience. So naturally, I am pushing Ruth to write her "story" as well. She has experienced lots of loss and has come out of it due to her choices to not let it bring her down. As a result, her story brings hope and encouragement for those who have had lots of loss and sometimes don't see how they can go on. I am so grateful that the Lord placed Ruth in my life and I look forward to more time with her.

Always be open to the people whom He brings into your life. You truly never know how they will affect you and maybe cause some changes in your perspectives of life. Stay open and show up!

CHAPTER 30

FINALLY FLOURISHING

*Oh, the depth of the riches both of the wisdom and
knowledge of God! How unsearchable are His judgements
and unfathomable His ways! For who has known the mind of
the Lord, or who became His counselor? Or who has first
given to Him that it might be paid back to Him again? For
from Him and through Him and to Him are all things. To
Him be the glory forever. Amen.*

ROMANS 11:33-36

When deciding what to title my story, I chose the word *flourish* because I loved that word. I thought it had a flair to it. It
wasn't just "prosper" or "thrive." It was a word that not many
people use. When sharing with a few friends that the Lord
wanted me to write a book, one of the girls who was all for it
said, "Kay, with all you have been through, it is truly a miracle
how you have seemed to 'thrive' through it all." I was contem-
plating that and knew for a fact that the only reason I didn't
end up with mental and addiction problems was because my

roots and my foundation were in the Word of God. His Word has been there for me at all times. I knew that on my own I would never have been able to move forward with any of the incidents that happened to me if I hadn't had "His word hidden in my heart" (Psalms 119:11).

No experience I have had has been futile and without fruit. His Word, like Him, never changes.

It is the same during good times and bad times.

"He has magnified His Word above His name" (Psalms 138:2).

"In the beginning was the Word, and the Word was with God" (John 1:1).

In trusting that He, being the Father, Son and the Holy Spirit, is with me in all I go through, then I know that I am never alone. Even when I don't want Him to see what I have done or walk alongside me, I still know that He is there and will always be there, not to shame me, but to remind me that He loves me with an everlasting love that surpasses all I do or don't do.

As I have shared my life story, most will agree that it is not that much different from most on this planet. I may have had more opportunities and advantages than most because of the time and place where I was planted, but there are still the trials, tribulations, joys and exhilarations. Some have had it easier and some much harder. One thing that defines the reason that I can say "life is good" is that I know personally the Lord Who is over it all. He guides me and is with me through it all. I know that He has given all of us choices, making us co-creators with Him.

I have chosen to see my heart and my life as a garden. One of my favorite movies and books is *The Shack* by Paul Young. In *The Shack*, the main character, Mack, has come to a place where he has to reconcile his faith to the fact that his youngest child has been murdered by a serial child killer and yet he blames himself. He actually gets to unload all his anger and guilt to God the Father, the Son and the Holy Spirit. It has a lot of symbolism relating to our relationship to the Trinity and how it all fits in with the ups and downs of this life we have here on earth. Mack learns that God never forces us in our choices. He gives free will to all to make healthy choices to enhance life or destructive ones that bring lots of pain. Another important part in the story is when Mack goes to spend time with Sarayu, the Holy Spirit, and she shows him a garden, which he thought should be a perfectly manicured one. He was confused when all he saw was chaos in the garden Sarayu seemed to be so proud of. As Mack communicated with Sarayu:

"Looks like a mess to me," muttered Mack, under his breath. Sarayu stopped and turned to Mack, her face glorious. "Mack! Thank you! What a wonderful compliment!" She looked around at the garden. "That is exactly what this is – a mess." "But," she looked back at Mack and beamed, "it's still a fractal too." Earlier Sarayu defined what a fractal was. "A fractal … something considered simple and orderly that is actually composed of repeated patterns no matter how magnified. A fractal is almost infinitely complex. I love fractals, so I put them everywhere" (*The Shack*, Paul Young, pg. 134).

Mack continues to help Sarayu toil in her garden as she hums a lovely tune that Mack enjoys. He starts to see the beauty in what they are doing together and he starts to "feel strangely at home and comfortable here" in her garden. Sarayu speaks to Mack, "And well you should, Mackenzie, because this garden is your soul. This mess is YOU! Together, you and I, we have been working with a purpose in your heart. And it is wild and beautiful and perfectly in process. To you it seems like a mess, but I see a perfect pattern emerging and growing and alive – a living fractal" (*The Shack*, Paul Young, pg. 145).

This is what God sees in us. "A mess!" But in His infinite way of seeing us, there is no end to the possibilities of who we are and what we can become. I find this wonderful positivity in Who our Heavenly Father, Son and Holy Spirit are so comforting because He knows that we really have no true natural view of how He sees us. Once we get into the eternal and immortal view, according to Him, of whom we come, He will NEVER give up on us or leave us. During my journey, this view was ingrained in me from the very beginning with the accepting love from my parents and family and an ever deepening knowing of who God is from all of life's events, the good and the bad.

Life never just "happens" to us. It is all about our will and our choices. I believe that God is a good God and would never want us to come to any harm much less make it happen Himself. As Jesus said in John 10:10, "The thief comes only to steal, kill and destroy. I came that they may have life and have it abundantly." When I go through events that pain me to the core, I look up to Jesus, the Father and Holy Spirit and know without a doubt that I have the "Three in One" with me, holding my hand and bringing me to the Light. This is a choice that I haven't always made. Sometimes we get to bad places where bad things happen to us and as a result we make bad choices. What I have learned in my story is that because of disappointments, the loss of dreams and sometimes someone else's choices, I get stuck, feeling alone and have a need to fix whatever "I" can to "make it all better." Whereas, maybe if I would let go and let God do His thing, then there is likely to be a better outcome. But no matter what, all three of the Trinity are with you, just like I truly believe that God the Father never left His Son's side during His darkest moment when He surrendered to the choices of his enemies, the Jews, the Gentiles and the whole world.

Once I came to this truth deep down inside of me, I have been able to see my life in a whole new light. During my down times and because of my heart beliefs, I lacked the power to overcome. Now I have learned that the power that is free and unbounded is the power that is in His Word. The only way to life and answers is through His Word. Jesus is the Word made flesh and He belongs to us.

As mentioned previously, the garden, the "mess" that Sarayu showed Mack is a great depiction of our lives. The Holy Spirit is there to work with us to get in there and chop down and weed to bring our lives into a "flourishing" garden. This is what the Father has in store for us. A "flourishing garden." This garden is a team effort between us and the Trinity. We have been invited to be a part of this team and experience this loving relationship. They truly want a deep knowing inside of each of us that we are all connected into this relationship. God's desire is that our life be a beautiful garden, full of life-giving sustenance to anyone who walks through it. As we walk in this world and live the life that God has brought to us through His Spirit and His precious Son Jesus, we are challenged to show this world that in Him there is a positivity and hope-filled life to share with others. The people who are watching our lives, as believers, are looking for that hope and optimism, and connectivity. This desperately hopeless world is crying out for life with the Trinity. We all want to "go home," just like Dorothy in *Wizard of Oz* states, "There's no place like home."

> *"Before I formed you in the womb I knew you*
> *and before you were born I consecrated you."*
> JEREMIAH 5:1

> *"For Thou didst form my inward parts; thou didst weave me*
> *in my mother's womb. I will give thanks to Thee, for I am fear-*
> *fully and wonderfully made; Wonderful are Thy works, and*
> *my soul knows it very well. My frame was not hidden from*
> *Thee, when I was made in secret, and skillfully wrought in the*
> *depths of the earth."*
> PSALM 139:13-15

We all started out in the bosom of the Trinity long before we were born to this earth. In Him our lives can bear much fruit and flourish no matter what life brings to us. Our external experiences don't determine "our flourishing." We can go through "Hell" and still flourish. It is what is in our heart and what comes out of our mouth that determine our flourishing or our languishing.

Some other scriptures I have found that encourage me to watch my words are:

> *"Let the words of my mouth and the*
> *meditations of my heart be acceptable*

in your sight, oh Lord, my Rock and my Redeemer."
PSALM 19:14

*"Thy Word have I treasured in my heart
that I might not sin against You."*
PSALM 119:11

*"The good man out of the good treasure of his
heart brings forth what is good: and the evil man out
of the evil treasure brings forth what is evil: for his mouth
speaks from that which fills his heart."*
LUKE 6:45

"As a man thinketh in his heart so is he."
PROVERBS 23:7

We all walk a fine line between order and chaos in this crazy world we live in. Many people have fallen deep into chaos never to see any order in their life. Just living chaotically through their choices and mindlessly wandering making one bad choice after another, like those who are facing life with a mental illness. Then there are the many others who are so far on the side of order that there is no freedom to live a truly abundant life. Fear seems to be at the core of both these conditions. With the wisdom of God and truly believing in the power of the Trinity in your life, a wonderful and wholesome life is possible between chaos and order. When trust and relationship with this Trinity is the core of your being, all the resources of the Universe are at your disposal. There is "nothing that is too difficult for our God" (Jeremiah 32:17). Life will always bring tribulations, but with His wisdom, peace and love we can know that "all things work together for good"

(Romans 8:28) because we know deep down that "This" is not "It!" There is so much more.

As I have gotten older, I have looked back on my life … childhood, teens, young adulthood, marriages, children and aging … and I praise God because I know that He has been by my side during all these phases. There is a comfort in not feeling condemned but being loved through it all. On the other hand, I know some people who grieve because they know they did not choose to have a relationship with Him in their early years. They just didn't know or didn't want to know. There is joy in their hearts today because they do know that even though they didn't realize it then, He really has been there all the while holding them up and guiding them. It is a truly joyous day when a person sees that no matter if they thought they were alone in life or just rambling through it, that He has been there all along, the Father, Son and Holy Spirit, the Three in One.

I remember the days of old I meditate on all my doings
I muse on the work of Thy hands
I stretch out my hands to Thee
My soul longs for Thee, as a parched land.
Psalm 143:5-6

ACKNOWLEDGMENTS

Writing a memoir has never been something I thought I would ever do. In fact, it was something I basically was loath to even consider. Throughout the Covid experience I received the call to write this. It would have never happened without the encouragement from our friend, Gary. So, Gary, I want to thank you first for being so sensitive to the Holy Spirit to deliver the message to me.

During the process of stretching my mind and trying to remember things I would have rather forgotten, was my mother, Marjorie, who remembered so much that I had forgotten.

I would never have gotten through the writing this on my computer without the skill and patience of my daughter, Lisa.

Last but certainly not least to my husband, ML. He has seen my tears uncovering old memories and provided the emotional support to keep me going. There were times when the whole process would hit a snag, and because of his encouragement I would trust the Lord through it all because this whole idea was His. Also thank you so much for taking old family photographs and making them shine.

None of this would be unfolding without the One Whom I have known through it all and am so grateful for His presence. This book has been a joy for me to complete. To the Father, Son and Holy Spirit, I give all glory and honor.

KAY WHITAKER was born in Fort Worth, Texas. She is a fifth-generation native Texan. Kay graduated from Texas Christian University in 1974. Growing up she lived in several different locations due to her father's occupation. Becoming a Christian at an early age, she depended on her faith to see her through many times of adversity. She worked as a teacher, and then later in life became a Registered Nurse - her dream job. She has been retired for 14 years, and recently felt the call and challenge from the Lord to share her story.

For speaking / media inquiries or to learn more,
please scan the QR code below,
or visit: https://flourishbecause.com